MW00834252

INNOVATIVE

INTERVIEW QUESTIONS
YOU'LL MOST LIKELY BE ASKED

250
Interview Questions

VIBRANT
PUBLISHERS

INNOVATIVE

INTERVIEW QUESTIONS
YOU'LL MOST LIKELY BE ASKED

Paperback ISBN 10 :   1-949395-97-9
Paperback ISBN 13 :   978-1-949395-97-6
Ebook ISBN 10:   1-949395-98-7
Ebook ISBN 13:   978-1-949395-98-3

Library of Congress Control Number: 2020938737

This publication is designed to provide accurate and authoritative information in regard to the subject matter covered. The Author has made every effort in the preparation of this book to ensure the accuracy of the information. However, information in this book is sold without warranty either expressed or implied. The Author or the Publisher will not be liable for any damages caused or alleged to be caused either directly or indirectly by this book.

Vibrant Publishers books are available at special quantity discount for sales promotions, or for use in corporate training programs. For more information please write to **bulkorders@vibrantpublishers.com**

Please email feedback / corrections (technical, grammatical or spelling) to **spellerrors@vibrantpublishers.com**

To access the complete catalogue of Vibrant Publishers, visit
www.vibrantpublishers.com

Table of Contents

Chapter **1**   Leadership   5

Chapter **2**   Personality   17

Chapter **3**   Confidence   51

Chapter **4**   Character   57

Chapter **5**   Adaptiveness   75

Chapter **6**   Composure   85

Chapter **7**   Behavioral   93

Chapter **8**   Innovation   111

Chapter **9**   Problem Solving   123

Chapter **10** Job Competency   131

Index   151

Dear Reader,

Thank you for purchasing **Innovative Interview Questions You'll Most Likely Be Asked.**
We are committed to publishing books that are content-rich, concise and approachable
enabling more readers to read and make the fullest use of them. We hope this book
provides the most enriching learning experience as you prepare for your interview.

Should you have any questions or suggestions, feel free to email us at
reachus@vibrantpublishers.com

Thanks again for your purchase. Good luck with your interview!

– Vibrant Publishers Team

1

Leadership

Personality

Confidence

Character

Adaptiveness

Composure

Behavioral

Innovation

Problem Solving

Job Competency

001. **Have you had the sole responsibility of bringing about changes in a company's organizational processes, or did you accomplish this type of change as the member of a team?**

Answer:

The correct answer to this question should shed insight on how the candidate led the company he worked for to bring about change in the way a company does business in response to changing market conditions.

As an example:

I have always endeavored to work within the framework of a team. An individual can make mistakes he is unaware of. When several minds work together, many potential errors can be detected before a process is compromised. Only in emergency or unusual circumstances should an individual work by himself on important projects.

002. **If you had sole responsibility for bringing about organizational change, how did your co-workers respond to the changes you were trying to bring to the company's organizational processes?**

Answer:

This question examines the candidate's ability to provide leadership under challenging conditions. The correct answer should provide concrete evidence of the candidate's ability to provide leadership.

As an example:

When an individual works on a project without collaboration, the people who will be required to implement the project or changes usually have doubts about the validity of the changes that are being implemented. Great caution must be exercised when business realities place the responsibility on the shoulders of a single person.

003. Are you able to make a judgment as to whether it is better for an individual or better for a team to bring about organizational changes?

Answer:

The correct answer to this question asks the candidate to make a value judgment. An interviewer will also make a judgment as to the value of the candidate's answer. The answer provided by the candidate will provide insight to the thought processes of the person applying for the job.

As an example:

It is always better for organizational change to come through a committee or a team. Teamwork goes a long way in alleviating troubles that can arise later in a process.

004. As a leader, manager, or supervisor, what creative methods have you personally developed to motivate your subordinates?

Answer:

The correct answer to this question requires the candidate's response to include some reference to recognized motivational theory such as needs, values, or goals.

As an example:

Current motivational theory teaches us that in today's workplace, financial bonus campaigns have less of a motivational factor than it did just a few years ago. Intrinsic motivation that enhances an employee's personal prestige or image of himself may have a far greater impact than paying a huge bonus. A bonus is spent and gone, but an employee who feels good about his work will be motivated to work even harder.

005. What methods have you developed to motivate employees to accomplish undesirable tasks?

Answer:

The interviewer is looking for concrete evidence of how the candidate is able to apply motivational theory in practical ways. The correct answer must show the interviewer that the candidate is able to successfully apply motivational theory.

As an example:

The best way to motivate workers to accomplish undesirable tasks is to simply help workers understand how beneficial the results will be, and that you will do your best to ensure every worker in the work center will have an equal opportunity at accomplishing undesirable tasks. There must be equality in scheduling workers to do jobs nobody wants to do.

006. When faced with a subordinate or a peer who is vocally unhappy about accomplishing an undesirable task, what methods have you discovered or developed to mitigate the dissatisfaction and to encourage the person to get the job done?

Answer:

This question seeks to gain an understanding of how the candidate would deal with undesirable workplace situations.

Correct answers to this question will provide insight on how well the candidate is able to respond to serious job complaints.

As an example:

Dissatisfied workers who vocalize their complaints are a real problem in most workplaces. In the first place, you must enforce that complaints must be vented through prescribed protocols. Spreading dissatisfaction to other workers is not acceptable. Secondly, dissatisfied employees must be taught the importance of completing the task that is causing the disruption. This process can only be completed so many times before a complaining employee may find their job in jeopardy.

007. How can company leadership become proactive in identifying employees who have creative talents that would benefit the company?

Answer:

The correct answer must address the different methods a company might use to identify and encourage talented employees to express their creativity.

As an example:

Companies trying to encourage employee creativity are an organizational culture that fosters creativity and company leadership that is committed to supporting the creative efforts of employees. If a company does just these two things, they will encourage creative employees to come forward.

008. As a manager or corporate officer, have you ever asked the question, "What is our company really good at?"

Answer:

The correct answer is "yes," alongside the appropriate level of explanation.

As an example:

This question addresses the core essence of every company in the country. What exactly does your company do best? The candidate should be able to provide real examples of how they have led a company to focus on the process that made them a leader in their industry.

009. Have you ever asked the question, "What are our company's core competencies?"

Answer:

Again, the correct answer is "yes." The candidate should understand what the core competencies are of the business they are working for. Core competencies are defined as a skill set that sets a company apart and gives it a competitive advantage.

As an example:

Core competencies are the foundational values that define a company. If a company is wandering off course, it is appropriate for people within the company to step up and say we have moved away from the things that brought us to this point, and must be depended upon to take us into the future.

010. As a leader, how do you think your subordinates perceive your personality?

Answer:

To answer this question correctly, the candidate will need to exhibit some transparency. What people think about us may not always be flattering. But for a leader, it is not always possible to be popular.

As an example:

The answer may include the thoughts that some people do like me as a leader, and some people have been very unhappy with some decisions I have made. As a leader I am required to balance the needs of the organization, the needs of the employees and the needs of the customers.

011. As a leader, how do you respond to rapidly changing business requirements?

Answer:

Change is the one constant that businesses must learn to work with. As an effective member of an organization's team, I must learn to change my approach to my job as market conditions change.

As an example:

A recent change in a regulation concerning the disposal of our company's waste products will require us to do a better job of ensuring potentially hazardous waste is properly collected and disposed of. Instead of complaining, I need to take the lead and make sure the regulations are complied with.

012. Can you tell me about a leadership decision you would like to change now that you have had time to think about it?

Answer:

To answer this question correctly, the candidate will need to do an honest reflection back to a problem that would have had a better solution if the candidate had done things differently.

As an example:

Years ago, I was faced with a decision to go forward with a business acquisition that had the potential to increase my company's profitability significantly. Because of the financial risks associated with the acquisition, I decided not to go forward and make the transaction. Another company took advantage of the opportunity, and it took us years to recover the competitive advantage that we lost.

013. As a manager or leader, have you had to work on an unexpected assignment over the weekend when you already had plans? How did you handle that situation?

Answer:

If the candidate has worked in a leadership position very long, the answer will be a resounding yes. Most people in leadership are asked to work beyond their normal hours to ensure important projects are completed on time. To answer the second part of the question, the candidate will need to provide a factual answer on how he handled the situation.

As an example:

I had plans with my family to go camping over the Fourth of July weekend. We had been planning on getting away for several weeks. During this time the company was trying to win a contract for a national advertising campaign. The client was not happy with the work that was presented to him and gave an ultimatum with an impossible deadline to fix the problem. My family was disappointed, but they knew my job was essential to keeping a roof over our heads, and they also knew there would be another weekend before the summer was over.

014. If you were in a group of about 10 executives, and you were asked to describe your leadership style, what would you say?

Answer:

The answer to this question may take any number of directions. Some leaders take an authoritative style, and some leaders take a style that is focused on building a consensus.

As an example:

My leadership style is best described as allowing the people who work for me to have sufficient leeway to express their own leadership and creative talents. I get involved when there are difficult decisions to be made that require executive authority to solve. I can be described as a facilitator.

015. How do you deal with the stress that goes along with being in charge?

Answer:

The correct response to this question revolves around the issue of knowing how to find a proper balance between responsibility and the need to take care of your own health.

As an example:

My workload is tremendous with seemingly impossible deadlines. Each day I take a few minutes away from my desk to get up and walk down to the break room, or to take a quick walk around the building. I try and laugh about my situation and try to have a smile for everyone who puts more work on my desk.

016. Since the time you moved into executive roles, what has been your most outstanding achievement?

Answer:

I was instrumental in improving health insurance benefits for the company I worked for.

As an example:

When the company hired me, only 50 percent of company employees were able to afford the company's health insurance benefits. During almost a year of intense negotiation with our insurance provider, I was able to negotiate a cost level that our people will be able to afford without causing them to reduce their overall quality of life.

017. As a company leader, have you ever held back from getting involved in an issue knowing you could have made a positive impact on the eventual outcome?

Answer:

Each candidate for the job may answer the question much differently. Some candidates may not have an experience where they held back when their input was needed. The interviewer is looking for a response that explains why the candidate did not get involved and what he will do differently if faced with a similar situation in the future.

As an example:

The company was having a real problem with employee retention and needs a solution that would work. After some other people came to me with some suggestions that would work, I still did not get involved. It took the company another six months to correct the issues that were causing the problems. My lack of action cost the company several thousand dollars.

018. How does your background in executive leadership make you qualified for this position?

Answer:

I have spent many years preparing in the effort to prepare myself to be a leader at the community college level. I believe my preparation makes me ready to step up into an executive leadership position.

As an example:

I have worked in virtually every administrative position there is in a community college setting. I have recently finished a PhD in educational administration, and I have been instructing business administration classes for over 10 years. I am now ready to assume even greater responsibilities as an executive.

019. Please tell me one area you need to improve in to become a better leader.

Answer:

Everyone has an area or two they can improve in, so I will share with you one area where I need to improve.

As an example:

I am not always as patient as I need to be with people who say things that do not make sense for me, or do not seem to fit the subject we are talking about. To make the necessary improvement, I need to become a better listener, and I need to make an effort to be more patient with comments that do not seem to make sense for the situation we are discussing.

020. Have you built up enough respect for your ideas that people at your last job actually came to you for suggestions?

Answer:

During the last year, I really began to feel that I was being recognized as someone who knew what she was doing.

As an example:

About two months ago the agency had the opportunity to earn a major contract, but there was stiff competition from two other companies. After several failed attempts to put together a proposal the client would accept, the boss came to me and asked for my opinion. I did have an idea that eventually was developed into a proposal that the client accepted.

2

Leadership

Personality

Confidence

Character

Adaptiveness

Composure

Behavioral

Innovation

Problem Solving

Job Competency

021. This question involves risks associated with taking advantage of a business opportunity. Without revealing sensitive personal information, can you describe a risk you have taken to gain an advantage in your business or profession?

Answer:

The correct answer will include a discussion of how a business risk the candidate took worked out well for the candidate's business or professional work.

As an example:

During a period when business was slow, an opportunity was available to take on a project that might be beyond your ability to complete within the parameters expected by the client. If you took on the project and failed to meet the requirements, your image would be   damaged, affecting your ability to be awarded similar projects in the future. In this case, you took on the challenging project and worked very hard to get the job done on time and done correctly, thus enhancing your image for potential clients.

022. Has risk-taking helped you grow professionally?

Answer:

This question requires a straightforward response that shows how risks have been beneficial to the candidate's professional career.

As an example:

The candidate is expected to discuss a risk taken at her job or in her profession that caused her to grow professionally or caused her to be more valuable to her employer. The candidate must discuss how she is more productive because of what she has learned through risk taking. Please cite examples of how taking calculated risks have helped you to grow in your profession.

023. Can you say if taking a risk has made you a more creative person?

Answers:

This question on risk taking is designed to develop an understanding of the candidate's ability to use creative thinking to solve difficult problems, or to respond to situations that require quick thinking.

As an example:

You developed a solution for a production problem that seemed impossible to solve. If your solution failed, it risked shutting down the entire production line. The answer the candidate provides must address the issue of whether or not the risk they took, and its success, caused them to develop creative skills they did not know they possessed.

024. Do you feel the current trends in organizational structure provide sufficient leeway for executives and managers to develop structures that meet current and future needs of businesses operating in the global marketplace?

Answer:

In this question, the interviewer is seeking information on the candidate's ability to creatively bring about change to the organizational structure of a company. This question is not challenging the candidate's record of success but is asking the candidate to think about how organizational structure and organizational processes can stifle creative thinking.

As an example:

> *I believe that current trends in organizational structure being developed by researchers at universities will enable organizations of all sizes to meet current and future challenges. In many cases, professional consulting agencies can be employed to help your company modify any of the new organizational structures to meet your company's needs.*

025. How would you describe or define workplace creativity? Provide concrete examples if possible.

Answer:

In this question, interviewers are more concerned with the quality of the answer. The correct answer must include concrete examples that clearly describe workplace creativity.

As an example:

> *Workplace creativity is the ability to look at a problem or issue and come up with a solution that enables the company to maintain market share and profitability. The creativity displayed by employees is the most important competitive advantage a company can possess. Competitive advantage is the engine of business profitability in the 21st century. An example might be a customer service process that is improved through the ideas workers bring to company management.*

026. How would you describe or define workplace innovation? Provide concrete examples if possible.

Answer:

Innovation is defined as the process of designing a new way of doing a job or task. A correct answer must include a response from the candidate that follows this definition.

As an example:

An example of innovation in my own professional experience is finding more efficient methods of responding to customer complaints. Every customer complaint should be addressed immediately when it is voiced, and a solution should be found that protects the relationship that exists between the customer and the company.

027. How would you describe or define workplace inventiveness? Provide concrete examples if possible.

Answer:

To correctly answer the question, the candidate should include use of the words devising or creating.

As an example:

An example of inventiveness in my own professional experience involves finding a way to improve a manufacturing process in order to bring increased product value to the finished product. Inventiveness may include redesigning workstations and machine tool processes or finding ways to get value for recycled waste materials.

028. In your opinion, how do effective communication skills play into workplace creativity?

Answer:

To correctly answer the question, the candidate should be able to tie the different types of communication to creative efforts.

As an example:

Effective communication includes face-to-face contacts, email, phone conversations, and interoffice memos. Without effective communication, an organization will not be able to complete its mission. Workers and employees must be trained to employ every communication protocol available for use.

029. Do you feel workplace creativity can be taught?

Answer:

The candidate should use educational and training experiences from his own professional growth to share how a person's creativity is enhanced.

As an example:

Almost every person in the workplace can be taught to make far greater use of the skills they bring to the workplace. People can be taught to think more clearly, be more efficient, and learn how to get more out of their personal passions.

030. If you feel workplace creativity can be taught, what types of classes or activities can be used to accomplish the training?

Answer:

This is a question designed to gauge the candidate's viewpoints of leadership in regards to creativity. The interviewer needs to gain an understanding of how the candidate would bring about professional growth for employees in the workplace.

As an example:

Employees can attend leadership training classes, college and university classes, on-the-job training, and be mentored by skilled people who have already proven their creative skills to the company.

031. How do you feel workplace creativity influences customer satisfaction?

Answer:

The candidate's answer should show how he would use creative activity to drive customer satisfaction.

As an example:

A very simple procedure I developed to enhance customer satisfaction was implementing a supervisory follow-up system that required a supervisor to call dissatisfied customers to ensure customer service representatives were able to satisfactorily resolve the complaint. Supervisors were given the discretionary authority to go beyond normal procedures to solve persistent problems.

032. In what ways can increased employee creativity improve a manufacturing company's productivity levels?

Answer:

The correct answer should include a discussion of how the candidate views the relationship between productivity and innovation.

As an example:

Employers who provide incentive for employees to submit their ideas can realize significant improvement in manufacturing efficiency ratings. The people who are doing the work often see ways to improve workflow that engineers miss.

033. How important is employee creativity to businesses operating in the global marketplace?

Answer:

This question examines the candidate's viewpoint on the relationship of ideas to the workplace. The correct answer to this question will show how the candidate contributed to a steady flow of new ideas and product development.

As an example:

Over the last 10 years I have worked in the new product development department at XYZ manufacturing company. I was responsible for conducting research that would lead to a constant flow of updates for the company's premier line of audio equipment. I believe my efforts enabled the company to maintain a 25 percent market share in the global audio equipment industry.

034. Do you think workplaces that encourage creativity are less stressful places to work?

Answer:

Creativity is an important element in the effort to relieve workplace stress. The interviewer is looking for candidates that have an understanding of the importance of creativity in relieving workplace stress.

As an example:

The candidate should provide a response that shows his understanding of how allowing workers to express their creativity can eliminate stress. Workers are tied exclusively to monotonous duties, and they are allowed to bring their own ideas for improvement and development to the discussion table. The candidate's answer may include a discussion of the idea that workers may have a need to be rewarded for bringing creative ideas to management's attention.

035. Do you consider creativity a skill, a talent, or a little of both?

Answer:

This is a question that expects the candidate to provide and answer based on a personal opinion. The correct answer will depend on the official position of the interviewer or the company he works for.

As an example:

Creativity can be described very simply as the ability to do or say something original. Creativity can impact communication skills such as a comedian putting together a brand-new comedy routine. Creativity, skill, and talent intertwine when a person brings forth his ideas in ways that are beneficial to his business or his professional life.

036. What is your definition of skill?

Answer:

The definition of skill includes the words proficiency, ability, capacity and aptitude; the ability or capacity to do a task proficiently.

As an example:

The candidate shares examples of her proficiency at a particular task such as her ability to quickly scan a document a subordinate has typed and find errors that need to be corrected. It may be that the candidate herself can type 60 WPM with 99 percent accuracy.

037. What is your definition of craftsmanship?

Answer:

A person who is very skilled at a particular trade. A craftsman displays the highest level of professionalism.

As an example:

The candidate worked in a cabinet shop and was responsible for designing and building prototypes of new products that would be displayed in the showroom. The candidate is a skilled cabinet maker who displays high levels of craftsmanship.

038. What is your definition of talent?

Answer:

The natural ability to accomplish artistic or creative endeavors. Talent may be thought of as superior ability.

As an example:

From an early age I have been able to play the most complex music ever written for the piano. As I have grown older, I have begun composing my own music, and have sold several pieces that have been used on the concert stage.

039. With sufficient training, do you feel a skilled worker can develop a real talent for a particular task or job?

Answer:

This question is designed to solicit an opinion from the candidate on the relationship between training, skill and talent.

As an example:

Over the last 10 years as the training manager for a large commercial glass company, our training program has been instrumental in the enhancement of our workforce to install glass on high rise buildings. I believe training is an essential element in the development of the skills a worker already possesses.

040. In some workplace situations, employees are closely supervised and allowed little opportunity for individual initiative. In your opinion, are there ways an employee can display creativity in this type of workplace?

Answer:

The correct answer to this question seeks a response from the candidate on the opportunity for employees in closely controlled work environments to find ways to develop their own ideas on how things should be done.

As an example:

Businesses that stifle creativity are usually more concerned with the daily operations that have proven to be profitable than in innovations that may challenge the way things have always been done. Even with operations that have been proven to work effectively, there is always room for a new idea. Employees working in an environment that is not receptive to change must look for subtle ways to get their ideas through resistant supervisors. This may happen when a disruption in a process occurs, and the only way to get things going again is to find a new way to fix the problem.

041. How do you feel your employers have viewed or judged your creative efforts?

Answer:

In order to answer this question correctly, the candidate will need to provide some quantifiable evidence that supports how employers judged his creative efforts.

As an example:

Last year, I received the company's highest award for innovation in employee recruitment and retention. Retention rates over the last year were up 75% from previous years. As a result of my efforts, I received the highest bonus the company has ever paid to someone not part of senior management.

042. It is possible to objectively identify a person with special talents or creativity?

Answer:

This question may be difficult for many to answer. Since everyone looks at creativity from a slightly different angle, what is creative in one person's mind may not seem very creative to another. To answer the question correctly, the candidate will have to be candid with the interviewer concerning their own view of creativity.

As an example:

Some people will sit at their desk and doodle on a piece of paper when they have spare time. Some of this artwork may look very good, and it may seem the person has a real talent as an artist. But if this person's artwork has no relationship to the work he is doing for the company, the perception by managers may be that this person is a time waster. In the business sense, it is much easier to identify real talent or creativity if the person's creative efforts are focused toward innovations that help the business.

043. Do you think the phrase "thinking out of the box" relates directly to workplace creativity?

Answer:

This phrase relates to a worker's ability to use thinking processes that would extend beyond the limits most people would not cross. To answer this question correctly, the candidate will need to address the validity of the assumption that "thinking out of the box" is a normal creative function that would be welcome in many work centers.

As an example:

If you believe there are situations that happen in business that require employees to reach beyond normal channels to solve problems that come up, you may be someone who would relate "thinking out of the box" to innovative thinking. If you think of this phrase as describing someone who is able to come up with new ideas at critical moments, then you might think of this type of person as someone who is using creativity to solve workplace problems.

044. In your opinion, would you consider yourself innovative or creative, and if so why?

Answer:

This is a question that asks for a subjective opinion and personal insight.

As an example:

There is a wide range of possible answers depending on the outlook of the candidate. The interviewer will be looking for a confident response that gives an indication of what the candidate thinks of his or her own level of creativity. An interviewer will be expecting the candidate to provide a definite example of creativity.

045. Do you feel there is too much or too little emphasis placed on the issue of creativity in the modern workplace?

Answer:

The correct answer should be a resounding no; there is not too much emphasis on creativity. Creativity is the life blood for businesses in the 21st century.

As an example:

A great example at this point would be Apple computers. Apple has used the creativity of its people to bring an unimaginable level of creativity to the electronics market. Every company dreams of having people that would allow them to obtain the same level of success that Apple has enjoyed.

046. What would you consider are some risks that come from being considered a creative person?

Answer:

The correct answer will include some thoughts of how other people may be jealous of a very creative person. The creative person may get most of the glory for what is being accomplished.

As an example:

Aside from experiencing some jealousy from coworkers, there may be a risk of being called upon to do more and more. An employer may depend on a creative person to the detriment of his family. Another consideration is that there may be tendencies to become a workaholic as the personal attention you receive becomes more and more fulfilling.

047. Do you think creative people are self-confident?

Answer:

The correct answer is "not always." Creative people are just other people in society. They have the same challenges in life that can cause a person to doubt the wisdom of a course they have decided to take.

As an example:

There are some creative people who are very self-confident in their ability to respond to their work requirements. There are other creative people who are not very secure in their response to their work requirements. This is not really different than other people who are not involved in creative efforts at their job. Ideally, employers are looking for confident workers at all levels.

048. Is it possible for a shy person to begin displaying a creative skill under certain circumstances?

Answer:

The correct answer is yes. Employers should be looking for ways to bring out the creative skills and talents of every employee.

As an example:

There may be an employee working at your business who has quietly gone about the business of doing his job without saying more than has been necessary to complete his daily tasks. At a certain point, difficulty in the work may arises that will require someone to come up with a new idea, and the quiet worker steps up and provides a great idea for solving the problem. The lesson is that we should never overlook the creative talents of any employee.

049. What kind of outside forces can cause an organization to become creative?

Answer:

The correct answer to this question should include a discussion of external forces that can threaten the stability of a business.

As an example:

External forces the candidate may discuss are competition, environmental disruptions, financial downturn, governmental regulation, and illegal activity. The candidate should be able to discuss an incident when one or more of these forces caused limitations on the creative efforts of one of her former employers.

050. Were you creative as a young child or a teenager?

Answer:

The answers that may be presented for this question will vary greatly. This question asks the candidate to reflect on how they viewed their life as a child or teenager.

As an example:

> *The person being interviewed should discuss times in their younger years when they were creative. The creativity may have nothing to do with the job being applied for. The interviewer is seeking an understanding of how the candidate developed the creative skills he has today.*

051. What kind of employer-based incentive do you support as a means to bring out creativity in employees?

Answer:

This is a question that is looking at a candidate's qualification for a leadership position. As a leader, the candidate may be in a position that requires her to bring out the creative talents of people who report to her.

As an example:

> *A candidate with several years of experience should have developed a viewpoint on the best methods for bringing out the creativity of a company's employees. Incentive programs that may be mentioned are bonuses, public recognition, promotion, and salary increases.*

052. Is there a creative business you would like to have for yourself?

Answer:

Possible businesses that may be mentioned include IT, cabinet shop, art studio, craft shop, ceramics, or a restaurant to name a few.

As an example:

The candidate's answer may include how serious he is about making his dream come true, and how he plans to realize the dream. The answer may have implications for the job the candidate is presently trying to get. The answer may also show the interviewer the candidate is able to dream big.

053. What historical figures do you consider very creative?

Answers:

The answer may include artists, engineers, business leaders, educators or other people who have accomplished great things for mankind. Even a political leader such as Abraham Lincoln could be on the list.

As an example:

Depending on who the candidate identifies, there should be a discussion of some factual details concerning the person's creative efforts. The interviewer should expect an answer with some detail and depth.

054. Which profession has the greatest percentage of creative people?

Answer:

The responses to this question will be subjective. Each candidate will have a different viewpoint on which professions are the most creative.

As an example:

Some candidates might provide an answer indicating their belief that artists represent the most creative profession. Another candidate might feel the most creative people are those who are designing the technologically advanced automobiles that are on the market. The point of the question is to get the candidate to provide some insight on how she views creativity in society and in business.

055. Do you think creative people are given unfair advantages at work?

Answer:

Answers to this question could elicit some strong responses. There may indeed be some candidates who believe that creative people do receive advantages that are unavailable to other workers. If the candidate is a creative person, he may feel the question is unfair and provide his own opinion of people who have such thoughts.

As an example:

The candidate who believes creative people receive an unfair advantage at work may be able to provide an example of a situation at their last job in which this happened. They may feel very strongly. On the other hand, creative people may feel the extra perks they have received have been justifiably deserved. A candidate with the correct position will affirm that businesses should maintain a balanced approach to rewarding creativity.

056. How important is it for senior leadership in a company to surround themselves with creative people?

Answer:

The correct answer is that leaders of any organization surround themselves with highly qualified and creative people to ensure the success of their organization.

As an example:

Depending on the level of the candidate, the candidate may express the viewpoint that he or she desires to be one of those creative individuals. On the other hand, if the candidate is trying to get into a senior leadership role, they should agree with the need to be surrounded by good people.

057. Do you feel your creative talents are great enough to develop ideas that will change the world?

Answer:

This question will allow the candidate to express his or her greatest aspirations. The correct answer is a response that shows the candidate can think about things that reach beyond the limitations of everyday life.

As an example:

The idea is to find an employee who will come to work and immediately begin the process of bringing dramatic improvement in the company's position in the marketplace. The company is not looking for mediocre performance, but outstanding contributions to the development of processes that increase profitability and market share.

058. What relationship does experimentation have to creativity?

Answer:

Experimentation does not necessarily lead to creativity. However, the result of experimentation may be that something new will be discovered.

As an example:

The candidate should provide a discussion of the ways experimentation can be used to support and develop creativity. Experimentation may simply be devoted to proving why some things do or do not work and can lead researchers down the path to new discoveries. To answer correctly, the candidate must show he knows the different paths that experimentation can take.

059. Are people conducting statistical research involved in creative activity?

Answer:

The correct answer may be a yes or a no depending on the candidate's personal viewpoint.

As an example:

Statistical research may be considered by some a technical activity that will not do anything considered creative activity. Others may consider statistical research a creative activity since the collection of data may uncover a truth that was not heretofore understood. The candidate should express an understanding that statistical researchers are also doing creative work under certain circumstances.

060. Do you ever get tired of being asked about creativity in job interviews?

Answer:

Yes and no. Creativity is important to business, but it is not always easy to brag about how creative I have been in my life.

As an example:

The candidate may provide a discussion of how she feels about her creative talents. The interviewer may be able to draw out some information about the candidate that was not provided on the resume. Every company is looking for the most qualified people that can be found. The candidate's creative tendencies may be the deciding hiring factor.

061. What is it about this job that will get your creative juices flowing?

Answer:

To answer this question, the candidate will need to know something about the organization's expectations.

As an example:

I have been studying the position I am being considered for very carefully. I am very excited about the opportunity to teach a full load of courses in the early American History department. I am particularly interested in the period from 1750 -1815. I know I will receive great joy helping students to understand the profound truths of equality and justice that are built into the founding of our great republic.

062. What would you like to say you have accomplished five years from now?

Answer:

The correct answer to this question is based on the specific goals the candidate has for his or her own life.

063. What would you like to say you have accomplished 10 years from now?

Answer:

My 10-year goal is to be in a senior leadership position in a software development company.

As an example:

I plan to get to a senior leadership position through continued growth as a software engineer. I plan to study hard and earn a doctorate level degree, and I plan to work my way up to a leadership position in a nationally recognized profession organization that supports and recognizes the work of software engineers.

064. How are the creative talents of a television news producer best developed?

Answer:

The correct answer should include a reference to a combination of education, training, and experience. As a producer works in the industry, she will increase her creative skills.

As an example:

The candidate may share information about some special news programs she has had the privilege to work with. The news programs were produced by a person who had been in the industry for many

years and was willing to teach a young producer many of the tricks
of the trade.

---

065. How would you describe the creative work of a television news anchor?

Answer:

A television news anchor has many opportunities for creative
expression. Each day a person in this type of job has the
opportunity to present the news in interesting and innovative
ways.

As an example:

*Many local news organizations advertise the important news in the
first 10 minutes of the broadcast. The idea is to provide people with
the news they are really looking for as quickly and as interestingly as
possible. This type of effort provides innumerable opportunities for
creative expression.*

---

066. Can you describe some ways a customer service representative can be creative in her job?

Answer:

A customer service representative is called upon on a daily
basis to creatively handle customer concerns and complaints.

As an example:

*A customer calls and says the electrical cord has pulled out of the
vacuum cleaner she just bought, and she only comes to town once a
month. The customer service representative must find a way to solve
this problem in a way that keeps the customer happy and at the same
time protects the bottom line of the company.*

067. What style of music do you enjoy the most?

Answer:

The answer to this question may not be exactly the same type of music the musician performs professionally.

As an example:

In her times of relaxation the musician may enjoy music that is very mellow, but professionally the person may be primarily involved in rock music. The answer provided will be an indication of the depth of the musician's musical range.

068. Is there a particular musician that you try to emulate?

Answer:

The answer to this question will provide the interviewer with insight into the musical foundation of the candidate.

As an example:

The candidate may name a famous composer such as Beethoven or may talk about a modern figure such as Paul MaCartney. Once again, the answer and the following discussion should provide valuable insight into the candidate's musical development.

069. Which musician had the greatest influence on your development as a professional musician?

Answer:

This question is asking for a slightly different response to the musician's development as a professional performer.

As an example:

Musicians may develop their own style based upon a particular musician they follow and enjoy. This development is an indication of where the candidate's career will go in the future.

070. Please describe what you would consider your ideal job.

Answer:

An ideal job may be something such as a chef, or a software developer, or a licensed contractor. The correct answer will be based on the type of job the candidate is applying for.

As an example:

The candidate may be able to describe a job as a software developer in which he has the opportunity to help solve a pressing problem in a developing nation. The nation is having a problem tracking the progress of a deadly mosquito borne disease. My work was instrumental in providing the software programs that every stakeholder in the fight could easily understand and use.

071. What would you say are the best things about your present position?

Answer:

This question asks the candidate to find something positive to say about his present job.

As an example:

When people work themselves up to justify leaving a job, they often build a much more negative picture than the situation really warrants. The interviewer is trying to force the candidate to find something positive to say about his last job. If the candidate cannot find something positive to say, it may be a disqualifying question.

072. Are there any buildings or structures in the world that you particularly admire?

Answer:

To answer this question correctly the candidate must describe a building or special architectural feature that actually exists. The candidate should be able to describe some of the structural features that make the building stand out in a special way.

As an example:

The candidate may say that he is particularly inspired by the Golden Gate Bridge. The candidate should be able to provide some numbers concerning the construction features or should be able to supply some information on why the bridge has withstood earthquakes and windstorms. Simply put, the candidate needs to provide a convincing discussion of why he is inspired by the building or structure.

073. Is there a current project this company is involved in that you would like to participate in?

Answer:

The correct answer may be yes there is. At the very least, all job candidates should have an idea what kind the projects the company is involved in.

As an example:

I am very interested in the new apartment complex this company is responsible for designing. This project represents exactly the kind of creative work I want to be involved in. I am very interested in designing projects that have a direct benefit to people.

074. Please describe your primary artistic interest.

Answer:

To answer this question correctly, the candidate must be able to describe a specific artistic discipline he is interested in.

As an example:

The artist may express an interest in oil painting or photography. The key is that the candidate must present enough information to prove to the interviewer that the artistic interest is genuine.

075. Can you describe your favorite artistic creation?

Answer:

To answer this question correctly, the candidate will need to effectively describe a work of art that she completed.

As an example:

The artist should be able describe her work with pride and confidence. It is important that other people can appreciate her work and understand the message she is attempting to communicate.

076. Do you have specific goals for your future endeavors?

Answer:

To answer this question correctly, the candidate should have some specific ideas about what he would like to accomplish in the short and long term.

As an example:

The candidate might say that in the short term I have two or three projects I need to get finished, and over the next few years I plan to learn a great deal more about western artists from the years 1860 to 1900. I trust that my studies will help me to communicate more fully the majesty of the American West.

077. Do you have any hobbies that are related to your work?

Answer:

The candidate should try and relate some things he does in his spare time that contribute to his overall ability as a creative person.

As an example:

I have taken hundreds of pictures of my family and friends. The latest digital technology has enabled me to create wonderful historical records of our family's annual gatherings. The photography I have taken with my family has directly help me as a professional photographer. I have learned a great deal about telling stories with pictures.

078. Can you tell me about a talent or skill you have that people would be surprised about?

Answer:

This question may generate some very interesting and revealing responses from the candidate. Most people can think of something they can do very well that only they know about.

As an example:

I am really good at changing brakes on cars. Most of the people I work with have no idea that I have excellent car repair skills. As I was growing up, my grandfather took the time to teach me how to use tools. We regularly worked on grandpa's cars. The ability to use my hands has helped me immeasurably as an artist.

079. At what age or stage in your life did you realize you had artistic talents?

Answer:

As a young child, my teachers were always getting after me for drawing pictures when I should have been doing my schoolwork.

As an example:

Very early in my elementary school days I began drawing pictures of birds. As I grew older and learned about different colors and artistic mediums, the quality of my pictures increased significantly. I eventually turned my artistic skills into a successful career.

080. Do you consider your work a form of communication, and if so, what kinds of messages are you trying to communicate?

Answer:

For creative people, the correct answer is yes. As a photojournalist I am trying to communicate the truth through my photographs.

As an example:

I have made a personal commitment to the truth. I do my very best to ensure that none of the pictures I take present an image that would deceive the public. Sometimes it is difficult to protect the truth. Yes, I said protect the truth. People in my position carry a very heavy responsibility to the truth.

081. How important is good grammar, vocabulary and spelling to an aspiring writer?

Answer:

The correct answer is the candidate agrees that he must have good grammar, vocabulary and spelling skills to be a good writer.

As an example:

One of the articles I submitted to my supervisor was rejected because I had made several spelling errors. I was very embarrassed and made a commitment that I would never turn in an article again until I had thoroughly proofread my work.

082. If we hire you for this position, what are some specific things you hope to accomplish?

Answer:

To answer this question correctly, the candidate needs to be very upfront about the goals he has for his work within the next year, and even for the long term.

As an example:

If you hire me for this position, my primary goal within the next year is to elevate the sports section of this newspaper to the number one position in the state. When people think about sports stories, I want them to think about us. In the long term, I believe we can hold the number one position in readership.

083. **If you have a choice, are you more interested in taking photographs that tell a human story, or are you more interested in photographs of nature and animals.**

Answer:

The answer to this question can follow two different tracks. The candidate may be more interested in human interest stories or may be more interested in nature. In either case, the interviewer will expect the candidate to tell a compelling story.

As an example:

I cannot resist taking photographs of children playing in an environment in which they feel safe and loved. The other day I was up in the mountains poking around in a campground when I came upon a family that was camped there. The family had four children, three boys and one girl. The kids all had their bicycles and were riding around the campground. I was able to get some excellent pictures of this family that I can use in an exposé on family summer fun in the mountains.

084. **Do you feel pictures have the power to sway public opinion?**

Answer:

I believe most definitely that pictures can tell the truth, or can be used to taint the truth, depending on the political leanings of the journalist or politician.

As an example:

One of the most compelling pictures of the late 20th century is the photograph of the nude Vietnamese girl running from a horrific scene of destruction from a battle. This photograph brought home to the American people the horrors of the Vietnamese conflict. These are the kinds of compelling pictures that photographers look for every day.

085. Is there a famous sports star that you would like to take a picture of?

Answer:

To answer this question correctly, the candidate should be able to identify at least one famous sports star he or she would like to get a picture of, and why.

As an example:

The other day I saw a well-known football star in the grocery store getting some things for his family. I was thrilled at the opportunity to get some pictures of this man going about his business just like everyone else. This man was gracious and allowed me to get his autograph for my son.

This page is intentionally left blank

3

Leadership

Personality

Confidence

Character

Adaptiveness

Composure

Behavioral

Innovation

Problem Solving

Job Competency

086. What skills or talents will you bring to the company if we hire you?

Answer:

To answer this question correctly, the candidate will need to discuss the particular skills or talents that make the person qualified for the job he is applying for.

As an example:

I am very skilled at designing software to meet the specific needs of small retail businesses. I have been very successful at designing and implementing systems that combine sales with ordering and inventory control.

087. Please describe the strengths you will bring to this company.

Answer:

To answer this question, the candidate will need to overcome his personal inhibitions and in a straightforward manner explain the professional strengths he will bring to the new position.

As an example:

I expect my work and the work of others to be of the very best quality possible. I will work very hard to make sure that every job I am assigned to do will be done correctly the first time. I am a very determined worker.

088. How do you think people perceive your music?

Answer:

The answer to this question requires a value judgment on the part of the candidate. It will be of interest to the interviewer to see how objective the candidate can be.

As an example:

The candidate may think that he has a large and loyal following, but in fact may not be very well known. On the other hand, the candidate may be modest and underplay his popularity. If the candidate is exaggerating or stretching the truth, the interviewer may need to keep looking for someone to fill the position.

089. How do you respond to live audiences?

Answer:

The only way a person can be a professional performer is to perform before live audiences, so a negative response to this question may quickly disqualify the candidate for the position she is seeking.

As an example:

If the performer is reluctant to perform before live audiences, she would be a liability to a band playing before live audiences or may be a liability to an orchestra. It may be possible for an instrumental musician to work professionally in a recording studio out of the public eye. The interviewer's needs are the key to correctly answering this question.

090. Do you consider yourself fully qualified on the latest advances in construction technology?

Answer:

The correct answer is yes. If the candidate is not qualified, he will be wasting the interviewer's time.

As an example:

I have done extensive study of the latest advances in the development of construction technology. Some of the projects I have been involved in the last few years have required me to use design features that could only be accomplished by using the latest construction advances. I plan to stay abreast of advances as soon as the experts prove them to be safe and effective.

091. How do you feel you should be compensated for your creative work?

Answer:

I believe I should receive the same level of compensation that people at an equivalent level in other industries receive. I am a professional with many years of experience.

As an example:

I believe my annual salary should be at least $48,000. I should not have to worry about my income being sufficient to meet my family's needs.

092. What character traits do you have that make you a great candidate for this position?

Answer:

The correct answer is that I have several positive character traits such as honesty, dependability, empathy and respect for everyone I work with.

As an example:

If you hire me you can depend on me being at work each and every day unless I am delayed by a cause beyond my control. I am committed to creating a respectful and just work environment.

093. If we hire you to work as a creative writer, what skills, talents and experience do you bring to the job that are more significant than other candidates have?

Answer:

The most significant skill that I bring to the table is my ability to see beyond the image that is immediately discernible. When I write a story, it will reach into the deeper motivations of the people who are involved.

As an example:

Last week there was a police officer shot when trying to break-up a gang related disturbance. I want to know some background on the police officer, I want to know more about the assailant, and I want to know why this particular neighborhood is experiencing gang related violence. There has to be an intense human-interest story somewhere in all of these human interactions.

094. How willing are you to have a coworker proofread your writing?

Answer:

I have made myself more receptive to allowing other people to read and be critical about the errors I make in my writing.

As an example:

Now that I have been in the business for a number of years, I usually work out an arrangement with a trusted coworker to allow her to look at my work and let me know where she feels I should make some corrections. It seems like an objective coworker can find mistakes you will never see yourself.

095. How do you rate your skills as a researcher?

Answer:

The best answer is that the candidate feels himself to be an excellent researcher.

As an example:

Over the past 10 years of being a professional writer, I have learned that my personal opinion has very little value in my writing. I have developed excellent library research skills, internet research skills, and I have become an excellent interviewer. My work will usually pass muster for its accuracy and reporting of the truth.

4

Leadership

Personality

Confidence

Character

Adaptiveness

Composure

Behavioral

Innovation

Problem Solving

Job Competency

096. **Many people are faced with times in their professional and personal life when they are required to take risks to get a project completed on time, overcome emergency situations, or take advantage of a business opportunity. Has there been a situation in your professional life when you had to take a risk to get an important project finished on time?**

Answer:

The correct answer will include a discussion of an actual event in which the candidate had to take a calculated risk to get an important task done by a specific deadline.

As an example:

In order to meet a seemingly impossible deadline, you had to assign a critical task to a team member who had not yet proven himself capable of completing any critical or essential tasks. If the unproven team member failed to get the task done when expected, you would fail to get the overall project completed on time, causing the loss of a profitable contract. In this case, you were able to help the unproven colleague finish the critical task on time, saving the contract for the company.

097. **What lessons have you learned about solving problems when faced with resistance?**

Answer:

In this question, the interviewer is trying to assess the candidate's creativity when attempting to solve problems that other people have not been able to solve.

As an example:

I have learned that people generally resist change. Change has to be sold to the people who must respond to the changes you must make to keep a company competitive. In our present competitive market environment, advances in technology are constantly requiring companies to change the way business is conducted. I was able to get all the wait staff at the restaurant I was managing to learn how to use all of the benefits and options of the computerized order placement system. This change reduced customer service time, significantly increasing customer satisfaction and company profitability.

098. Of all the projects you have been called upon to complete in your professional career, what would you say was your greatest creative achievement?

Answer:

This question is designed to allow the candidate to highlight a personal success she is proud of. The interviewer will be evaluating the candidate's ability to concisely communicate the value of her achievements.

As an example:

The project that I feel was my greatest professional achievement happened when I was able to write and develop a training routine that enables workers to safely handle liquid oxygen during a manufacturing process. The training process has now been implemented industry wide and should be the training standard for many years to come.

099. How important is it that your work on important projects be recognized by professional organizations?

Answer:

This question asks the candidate to quantify the value of their work in relationship to other professionals in the industry.

For many people, professional recognition is a valuable motivational factor.

As an example:

Recognition by professional organizations represents quantifiable evidence that the work you are accomplishing is recognized and accepted as valid. This validation of a professional's work is a significant motivating factor. Without professional recognition of a person's work, critical sharing of important research and development would be stifled.

100. **If you were an inventor, what kind of device or machine would you like to invent that would make people's lives better or would improve the human condition?**

Answer:

This question allows the candidate to share some of her dreams and aspirations. The way to answer this question is to show some enthusiasm for the dream you are expressing.

As an example:

A good example would be an idea that really seems plausible and attainable. It might even be the company the candidate is applying to can provide support for the development of the candidate's dream. This is a question that could spark a spirited discussion between the interviewer and the job candidate.

101. Do you desire to have your creative works recognized or publicly displayed?

Answer:

To some, answering this question may seem unfair, but the reason for the question is to find out if the candidate is prepared to take a leadership position in the technological or business advances that will take a company into the future.

As an example:

A candidate who is shy about facing public recognition or scrutiny may not be able to step up and take a strong leadership position when called upon to do so. Good leaders are not shy about public recognition, but they do desire that publicity be accepted in the correct attitude.

102. Would you be satisfied with your life's work if you never received any significant public recognition for the work you have accomplished? Please defend your answer.

Answer:

The correct answer is "no."

As an example:

Although there is a simple answer to the question, the interview will expect the candidate to provide some concrete support for their answer. The support should show the why or why not of the candidate's answer. The ideal candidate will desire some acceptable recognition of the things they have been trying to accomplish throughout their professional career.

103. Do you consider a machinist repairing a machine tool in a factory a creative person?

Answer:

The correct answer is "yes," alongside the correct level of explanation.

As an example:

A skilled machinist creates value for the factory he is working for when he is able to keep the machinery running. Running machinery keeps the factory profitable. Although a machinist does not wear a tie to work, or does not paint a beautiful picture, the conduct of his trade can be very creative. This type of question is designed to help the professional candidate broaden her understanding of creative work.

104. Is the auto mechanic who repairs your automobile a creative person?

Answer:

Going along with the question of the creativity of a machinist in a factory, the answer should be "yes," an auto mechanic can be a very creative person.

As an example:

An auto mechanic working for a NASCAR team is a very creative member of a team that brings happiness to all of the fans. A mechanic is creative when he is able to repair a customer's car in a way that saves money. They are also creative when he or she helps a young person learn their trade. The candidate should show an understanding of how people from all walks of life can be involved in a creative way.

105. Are engineers who develop software applications simply working as technicians, or are they people who are serving as creative experts?

Answer:

They are creative experts without a doubt.

As an example:

The great equalizer in the business world is the software that a company is able to use to create competitive advantage. Software that works effectively saves a company time and money, thus increasing the opportunity for increased profitability. Job candidates in today's corporate environment must embrace the full application of advanced technology.

106. What part of your job makes you wake up with anticipation?

Answer:

In order to answer this question correctly, the candidate should be able to convince the interviewer that there is something about their career that causes excitement for the candidate.

As an example:

In this case, the candidate would need to provide a discussion of something about his job that made him dream about going to work. The something could be a special project or could be a creative effort that will make a significant impact on his profession.

107. How important is safety in the workplace?

Answer:

Doing a job safely is the most important factor in any project.

As an example:

I believe there is no circumstance that would cause me to violate established safety standards when doing a job or working on a creative project. Safety trumps all other considerations.

108. How would you describe the creative work of a surgical nurse?

Answer:

A surgical nurse's day-to-day duties provide many opportunities for creativity. A surgical nurse's responsibilities begin hours before surgery and may last for many hours after seeing patients through the recovery process.

As an example:

A surgical nurse preps patients for surgery, provides information to family members, assists the surgeon, works in the recovery room, and presents a professional image to patients and their families. All of this work allows many opportunities for creative work.

109. How would you describe the creative work of a landscaper?

Answer:

A landscaper combines knowledge of construction, horticulture, and artistic design.

As an example:

*A landscaper takes the ideas of a potential customer and makes them
a reality that adds beauty and value to the customer's property.*

110. How would you describe the creative work of a police officer?

Answer:

A police officer is forced to find creative solutions to the
situations they are thrust into daily.

As an example:

*A police officer is called to a horrific accident scene in which a child
is trapped in a car and needs immediate help. The officer must
find a way to help the child, control the chaos, and comfort family
members who are frantic to get the child out of the car. Scenarios like
this provide innumerable opportunities to find creative solutions to
problems.*

111. How would you describe the creative work of a firefighter?

Answer:

A firefighter is primarily concerned with saving lives and
protecting property. In emergency situations, firefighters are
called upon to step into incredibly dangerous situations to
save lives.

As an example:

*A firefighter is called to a residential fire and learns there is a family
trapped on the second level. Firefighters must find a way to get into
the home and rescue the family at the least possible risk to the lives of
the firefighters.*

112. How would you describe the creative work of a welder?

Answer:

The work of a welder is creative from its very foundation. A welder takes two pieces of metal and creates something useful or decorative.

As an example:

A welder can take various pieces of steel and create a wrought iron fence, or a welder can join together a pipeline that brings oil to a refinery which refines all of the petroleum products that make our lives so much easier.

113. When you reach retirement age, what would you like to have people remember you for?

Answer:

I have thought a lot about what the end of my working career will be like. I would like people to remember me as a person who cared deeply about the value of his work and the people he worked with. I would also like my work to have a lasting impact on the environment.

As an example:

I have been working on projects that are focused on developing sustainable water projects for towns and villages in the Western United States. When my working career is over, I want to be able to leave behind a legacy of helping people through environmentally sound projects that protect the environment, and at the same time provide safe water to people in rural areas.

114. Are you good at sharing the applause with the other members of the group you are performing with?

Answer:

The correct answer to this question will provide the information on the willingness of the candidate to work as a team. One person in a group who is unwilling to share the accolades being received from the public may be a serious liability.

As an example:

The band is enjoying great success, and the lead singer is receiving far more recognition than the rest of the band. This can be a problem since the lead singer's success depends on the work of the entire band. The interviewer may be concerned that the cohesiveness of the band may be endangered when one member will not share the accolades from the public.

115. What is the greatest thing you hope to accomplish as a musician?

Answer:

The correct answer to this question will be an indication that the musician expects to grow professionally. The interviewer is looking for a response that provides some confidence that the candidate desires to learn more about music than he presently knows.

As an example:

Currently I perform with a local band and working to improve my skills, to sign as the lead musician with one of the major record labels in future.

116. Are you willing to perform for charity?

Answer:

The willingness to perform for charity may be very important to some musical groups. The correct answer is yes, I will perform for charity.

As an example:

The organization the candidate seeks to work with may have particular charitable interests that are very important to the organization's audience. In this case, the unwillingness to perform for charity would be a disqualifying answer.

117. Please tell me about the last book you read. What about the book did you find meaningful?

Answer:

This question seeks to elicit from the candidate a picture of the kind of books that may influence the candidate's life and work. The hope is that the answer to this question will provide the interviewer with some insight into the candidate's creative interests.

As an example:

The candidate should be able to describe a section in the book he has recently read that was particularly inspirational. The interviewer may try to draw out as much detail from the candidate as possible.

118. How would you define success?

Answer:

The answer to this question may go in many different directions as the candidate finds a way to define success according to her own understanding.

As an example:

Standard definitions of success contain words such as achievement, desired outcome, rewards of hard work, or becoming famous. The candidate's response should follow a line of discussion that contains the ideas expressed in these words.

119. Many times people in leadership positions do most of their important work away from the office. What do you think the people who work for you feel about your extended absences from the office?

Answer:

The correct answer to this question should be based on a recounting of all the valuable work the candidate does for the company by being out in the community keeping essential work-related relationships intact.

As an example:

The candidate is a member of several organizations that have a major impact on the ability of the city to meet the needs of every citizen. The relationships that are forged by being on the steering committees have created a business bond that has directly led to the continued profitability of the company.

120. Is there a special reason that you applied for this position?

Answer:

The answer the candidate gives for this question should reveal the motivations the candidate has for applying for the job.

As an example:

The candidate may see this job as the best opportunity she has to achieve her professional goals. The candidate may feel there are no other comparable opportunities anywhere else in the candidate's chosen profession. The question cannot be completely answered without some words justifying the candidate's reasons for seeking the job.

121. Why do you want to leave your present position and come to work for this company?

Answer:

Answering this question correctly may not be very easy. The candidate may be reluctant to reveal some of the reasons he is trying to change jobs. The interviewer must be careful not to pry into personal information he has no legal right to hear.

As an example:

There may indeed be a justifiable reason for the candidate to change jobs for professional advancement. On the other hand, there may be an issue at the former employer that the candidate is trying to escape. If the interviewer sees the potential in this candidate, he will do his best to find a balance between the company's need, and the caution that must be taken when bringing new people into the company.

122. **When do you think it's necessary for a leader to tell workers it is okay to violate established operating standards or procedures?**

Answer:

The correct answer for this question is founded in the principle that there are work situations that require a response that does not fit any prescribed procedures.

As an example:

If an emergency situation arises in a work center, the only way to respond quickly may be to overrule what most of the people think should be done. If a man slips and is dangling precariously from a safety strap, someone may have to risk their own safety to save the man from further injury. Under normal circumstances, there must be a great weight of justification before established rules should be overruled.

123. **Please discuss your viewpoint on the creative opportunities of a chef.**

Answer:

The chef must be able to establish a creative vision for her restaurant. What type of food will be on the menu? Will the restaurant cater to a very upscale clientele, or will the chef endeavor to reach a broad cross section of the public?

As an example:

The chef wants the menu to center around French cuisine, but with a strong emphasis on sea food. The chef will be interested in challenging restaurant managers to create an atmosphere in the restaurant that supports that image. People who come into the restaurant will expect to pay a little higher price but will enjoy an extraordinary dining experience.

124. Can you describe how a chef projects the image he is looking for to his staff?

Answer:

The chef's responsibility to communicate to his staff is not much different than a leader in any profession. Great chefs need to be great communicators. The success of a chef's restaurant depends as much on inspiration, as it does on the individual cooking skills of each member of the kitchen staff.

As an example:

The kitchen staff must be a cohesive team that is dedicated to preparing food that provides each patron with the best experience possible. The ideal outcome is patrons who walk away committed to returning to the restaurant with other friends in the very near future. The key to ensuring this success is a disciplined staff, an inspiring chef, a restaurant with a wonderful appeal and people who are happy to be working where they are.

125. Are there any new advances on the horizon that are particularly exciting to you?

Answer:

I am excited about handheld devices that allow me the opportunity to work anywhere I can get an internet connection.

As an example:

I have the latest edition of the iPod, and my productivity has improved significantly and my ability to communicate with my clients has been enhanced so significantly that I have reduced the instances of misunderstanding.

126. What has artistic expression brought to your life?

Answer:

Beauty, value, respect, love and an understanding of the emotions that control human interactions.

As an example:

I had to do the research on several human-interest stories over the years for a book I was commissioned to write. Through all of this work, I learned that the situations people find themselves in usually begin as a simple disagreement or misunderstanding.

127. As a photographer, what is there about a pristine mountain lake that would cause you to stop and take a picture?

Answer:

When I look at the scene you have just described I am usually moved very deeply by the beauty of the colors and the beauty of the different natural elements. Many times, I have no choice but to stop and start taking pictures.

As an example:

Pictures are the vocabulary of the photographer. The only way I can share such a scene with my friends or with the public is to shoot several different shots and put a story with each shot. There may be a buck over next to the tree that is so majestic with his velvety antlers, or there may be a gleam from the lake that sends shivers down your back. This is my reaction to the scene you described in your question.

128. If a photographer came upon the scene of a horrific auto accident, how important is it to stop and take some pictures?

Answer:

It is very important. The police might use the pictures to investigate some important elements of the accident, or the families of the victims may find the pictures useful in understanding what happened.

As an example:

I was out on assignment for the newspaper I was working for and came upon a fatal accident scene. The pictures I took provided the police with some essential evidence for determining the fault for the accident. Without my photographs, determining the guilty party would have been much more difficult.

5

Leadership

Personality

Confidence

Character

Adaptiveness

Composure

Behavioral

Innovation

Problem Solving

Job Competency

129. **In your experience, are there ways that the requirement to meet strict deadlines can cause you to become more creative?**

Answer:

The correct answer should show how the candidate can use project deadlines to become more creative in bringing a project to a successful completion.

As an example:

The only way that strict project deadlines can be met sometimes is to use all the modern technology that is available. As a newspaper reporter I have to be able to format pictures or graphic displays into my articles. Many times, I am forced to learn new applications for the publishing software I use on the job in order to get my work done on time. Strict deadlines have forced me to become better with the tools that I have available to do my job.

130. **Has there been a situation in your professional life when the requirement to meet strict deadlines stifled your creative efforts?**

Answer:

In this answer the candidate has a little latitude to express some dissatisfaction with a situation he found himself in. The candidate should be able to share how he overcame the limitations imposed by a strict deadline.

As an example:

As an architect, I am called upon to design some complex building projects. Constantly changing codes and design restrictions tend to slow or impede my progress on important projects. Clients can impose unrealistic deadlines that prove difficult to meet. If not dealt with properly, these obstacles make it very difficult to move forward with a creative project. I can only overcome these types of challenges through team efforts.

131. If you had a situation that made it difficult for you to be creative, how did you (or how did you not) overcome the difficulties related to that situation?

Answer:

The correct answer to this question will include a candid discussion of how the candidate overcomes obstacles.

As an example:

It usually is true that it takes a team effort to overcome obstacles. One person can only look at an issue from his or her own perspective, and when an insurmountable problem arises, it takes one or more other people to bring in different viewpoints. When faced with difficult situations, I always seek an opinion from a person who can bring a fresh and productive perspective.

132. In response to difficult situations, have you been able to develop some personal strategies for handling similar situations that you may face in the future?

Answer:

This question is designed to find out if the candidate can think under pressure, and if the candidate is able to learn positive lessons from difficult situations. The correct answer requires the candidate to show how he or she developed strategies for dealing with difficult situations.

As an example:

> *I try to learn from difficult challenges I have had to overcome, and
> I always make it a point to learn from my mistakes. I maintain a
> personal journal of all the challenges I am required to face in my
> professional life. Things that require me to learn new ways are
> highlighted. In this manner I have compiled an extensive list of
> methods that can be used to overcome challenges with my creativity.*

133. **As you think back on a failed process or project, have you
been able to determine why your creative efforts were not
sufficient to bring about a positive result?**

Answer:

This question asks the candidate to take her personal reflection
to the next level. The interviewer is looking for information
that shows the candidate has the ability to overcome failures.

As an example:

> *My creative efforts were not sufficient to bring the project to a
> satisfactory conclusion because I failed to collaborate with my peers
> as effectively as I should have. In the fast-paced market environment
> we work in today everyone in a position requiring high levels of
> creativity needs to be open to working as a team.*

134. **Successful project management requires managers to be able to look at the direction a project is going and find ways to adjust the project to bring about the expected results. Using a project or business process you have had control over, were you able to find ways to adjust the project to bring about the desired results?**

Answer:

The candidate should have the ability to look back on difficult projects and develop new improved creative abilities. It's the old adage; people need to learn from their mistakes.

As an example:

As a construction project manager, I was responsible for ensuring projects followed the critical path to completion. Every essential step is plotted on the critical path. When a problem arises that impacts the project's critical path, my responsibility is to bring to bear all the necessary resources to solve the problem and get the project back on track.

135. **Do budgetary limitations imposed by management limit your ability to bring forth innovative ideas?**

Answer:

There are times when budgetary limitations can restrain innovation.

As an example:

The need to budget money to pay for research and development may be difficult to fulfill during times of financial downturn. The problem with this scenario is that research and development is the basis of a company remaining competitive and profitable over the long term. The candidate should have a plan for helping a company overcome the budgetary limitations that can stifle innovation.

136. What was the most difficult challenge you ever had to face on the job?

Answer:

To answer this question correctly, the candidate will need to open up and share an experience that was very difficult and may even have had a negative outcome.

As an example:

I worked at XYZ company for 15 years and developed many close friends through my job. At the 15 year point I was promoted to a supervisory position. This placed me above many people I had worked with for many years. Over time, it became necessary for me to fire one of my old friends because of poor job performance. I had a very difficult time with this responsibility. My old friend departed the company with many bad feelings toward me.

137. Please describe how you would handle a project that had large amounts of conflicting information.

Answer:

In order to handle a project with significant amounts of conflicting information, you should use a graphic organizer to lay out all of the inputs in an organized manner.

As an example:

The information can be organized in a flow chart, or a Venn diagram. Regardless of which system is employed, it will be essential to discard or put aside any inputs that do not directly lead to the successful completion of the project.

138. How do you respond to interruptions when you are working on critical projects?

Answer:

Interruptions are a real problem when a person is working on a critical project. Even a minor interruption can set a project by many hours or days. The key to handling interruptions that interfere with completing your project is setting healthy boundaries with team mates, communicating with them that you are on a project which needs your complete focus.

As an example:

While working on a critical project, the client keeps calling me to ask how I am doing every two days. In order to mitigate the interruptions, I have assigned a trusted assistant to handle the client's calls. The assistant has all the necessary information available to him to ensure the clients questions are answered correctly.

139. When you are in the process of designing a building or major project, what are some things that hinder your progress?

Answer:

Unnecessary interruptions, being drawn away from my work to respond to nonessential duties and clients constantly coming in with additional requirements and changes.

As an example:

There are points during the creative process when interruptions can set an architect's work back by several days or weeks. The office staff needs to be sure and enforce the creative time of the architects assigned to important projects. I understand there are times when I need to be patient with interruptions, but there are other times that I need to stand my ground and insist on not being interrupted.

140. Have you ever had to collaborate on a complex project with colleagues in remote locations?

Answer:

Many architectural firms collaborate on projects all around the globe. The interviewer is interested in finding out if the candidate is comfortable with global communication systems.

As an example:

In my last position I collaborated on many projects the company was involved in overseas. The company was working on many projects in Asia, and I was gaining valuable experience with communication systems that allowed me to communicate with project managers face to face.

141. How does advanced technology help you as an architect?

Answer:

Architects must learn to use the latest technologies if they expect to remain relevant in their profession.

As an example:

Advances in technology such as computer aided design systems and advanced communications systems offer the best opportunity we have to increase our productivity. These technology advances are essential since economic realities have forced many firms to reduce support staff.

142. Have you been involved in a project in which you were not provided with enough information to do the job properly?

Answer:

Yes, I have been, and I had to work very hard for many days to get all the information I needed to accomplish the project.

As an example:

I was assigned a project to determine if our company's employee pay scale was competitive. I was asked to look at salaries from the lowest paid worker to the most senior executive. I had a difficult time gaining access to the salaries of the top company leadership. I eventually found the information I needed. I received positive recognition from my supervisors on the accuracy of my work.

143. In what ways has modern communication technology changed your job as a writer and communicator?

Answer:

The most significant change is the speed at which copy can be posted to the internet and seen by people all over the world. In the past it took time for printed materials to reach the audience. The transfer of printed work is almost instantaneous.

As an example:

I write and post a daily blog on my website. Within just a few minutes after my work is posted, I am receiving feedback on my comments. Not only that, I am receiving feedback from all over the country and even the world. The speed at which information moves across the globe is changing the very foundations of human interaction.

This page is intentionally left blank

6

Leadership

Personality

Confidence

Character

Adaptiveness

Composure

Behavioral

Innovation

Problem Solving

Job Competency

144. Can you think of a time when you designed a project or process for your business or organization and the project failed?

Answer:

People do not like advertising their failures, but in this case the interviewer is looking for the candidate to reflect on a project that did not go well.

As an example:

Recently I was put in charge of developing an updated mission statement for our organization. Although I felt I had put together a mission statement that would serve our organization well for many years, upper level managers completely rejected my work. As I reflect back on my efforts, I should have been more willing to allow my peers to review my work before I submitted it for approval to upper level management.

145. Please tell me of an instance when you were right, and the boss was wrong?

Answer:

The correct answer to this question will require the candidate to provide information on a real instance in which she was right, and the boss was wrong. The interviewer does not want to hear about imaginary situations.

As an example:

I had a disagreement with the boss over how to solve a customer complaint about a piece of equipment we had sold over the internet. The equipment had failed, and the customer wanted a refund or replacement of the broken machine. The boss was convinced the failure was the customer's fault, but I knew better. We had shipped the product with the wrong spark plug. I had to have the machine shipped back to us so I could prove to the boss that we had made the mistake and needed to respond properly to the customer's complaint.

146. Can you handle more than one creative project at a time?

Answer:

The interviewer wants to know how well you handle multi-tasking, particularly when it involves projects that require more thinking outside the box and potentially providing new ideas or methods. It may be more difficult for some to handle multiple projects that involve thinking outside the box, coming up with new ideas and solutions, and not following a set guideline. The interview wants to know you are able to prioritize and not feel too scattered when required to be more creative than normal.

As an example:

I enjoy creative projects where I have the freedom to introduce new concepts or come up with new ideas to solve problems. I mostly enjoy projects where I am able to create a product that is completely new. At my last position working in IT, I was able to take the reins on a new software line that our company was putting out. I already had been working on updating a new ERP system within the office, and was excited to be able to take over the huge task of creating a software that would be sold to our vendors the following year. I immediately began working on the new software, while creating a team to help finish up the existing project of updating our office ERP software. I was able to oversee the creative aspects of the ERP upgrade as well as complete the new software product on time and within budget.

147. How do you respond when you are accused of making a mistake on a critical project?

Answer:

The candidate may respond by saying he does not like being called on his mistakes. It may take a lot of justification to get the candidate to admit to an error.

As an example:

A critical project the candidate was working on ran into a significant snag. The other people on the team accused the candidate of making serious errors at a critical point in the project. In the face of substantiated evidence of the mistake, the candidate finally had to admit he had made a serious error in judgment.

148. How do you respond to emergencies or crisis situations?

Answer:

The correct answer is that the candidate has learned to handle emergencies in a calm and orderly manner.

As an example:

During the recent firestorms in our community, our main warehouse was at risk of destruction. Working with the emergency response personnel, we were able to develop a plan that saved our building from total destruction. Although we did suffer the loss of some of the products in the warehouse, we were able to salvage enough to meet the immediate needs of our customer base.

149. How do you respond to people who are yelling at you about a decision you have made?

Answer:

The correct answer is that I do not like it when people yell at me, but that kind of behavior does not produce any conducive response for either party.

As an example:

A few days ago, a person in the accounting department was very unhappy about an expenditure I approved. This person came into my office and expressed his displeasure with me in a very strong and loud voice. I asked the person to sit down and allow us to discuss the issue in a calm and mature manner. Due to my approach, we were able to solve the problem to our mutual agreement.

150. When you are required to move from project to project throughout the day, how does that affect the way you respond to co-workers and supervisors?

Answer:

The correct answer is that no matter how tough the day is, "I maintained a professional attitude toward all of my coworkers."

As an example:

In my position at the company, I am usually under significant pressure to respond to a multitude of tasks and projects. No matter how frustrating the situation becomes, I cannot lash out at anyone, or refuse to listen to the next issue that arises.

151. What is your response when a co-worker copies your work on a project and tries to take full credit for completing the project?

Answer:

The correct answer should include a statement that the candidate feels it is improper for coworkers to take credit for another person's work. With that said, the candidate should also display a level of maturity and composure in how they would respond to such a situation.

As an example:

If a coworker takes credit for something I have accomplished, I need to respectfully go through the correct chain of command and voice my dissatisfaction with the situation. If the infraction is minor, I might not say anything. Each case must be considered for its own merit.

152. When you are tired and don't feel like working, what do you do to keep yourself sufficiently focused to complete a critical task or project?

Answer:

The correct answer is the candidate develops some motivational strategies that create an attitude that, "I will not allow the difficulties of the day to keep me from completing my work to the best of my ability."

As an example:

There are a number of great strategies to keep you going each day. Get up and move around occasionally, find a way to laugh with a coworker, focus your thoughts on the importance of the job you are doing or think about how important your job is to yourself and your family. The challenge is that everyone should have a job they like and should have a job they feel is important.

153. When you are working on a long and difficult task that never seems to end, how do you keep yourself going all the way to the end of the project?

Answer:

The correct answer is that I must use all of my personal strategies for staying focused when working on difficult tasks or projects and then provide a few examples.

As an example:

There will always be occasions when a person is required to undertake difficult and time-consuming tasks at work. The jobs that can be done quickly are always the ones people want to undertake. The long hard jobs require the worker to do everything possible to stay focused on the finish line. You have to resist distractions, resist pesky coworkers and realize that when the job is done you will have a great feeling of accomplishment. You might set a little reward for yourself for successfully completing the job.

154. When you are given an overwhelming workload that must be completed by the end of the day, how do you respond?

Answer:

The correct answer is that you have to respond with a firm commitment that you will not allow yourself to become discouraged, and you need the courage to ask for help.

As an example:

> *Everyone needs to learn that employers depend on people who prove*
> *themselves able to get the work done when all others are standing*
> *around doing nothing. If you are a good worker, the boss is going to*
> *send the bulk of the work your way. When you are overloaded, you*
> *need to be courageous enough to ask for help. In some cases, there*
> *will be no other way to get all the work done on time.*

155. How did you react when your work as a writer was rejected by your supervisor?

Answer:

Most candidates will express some unhappiness about supervisors rejecting their work. The key to the correct answer is the attitude the candidate displays when discussing this question. My ideal response is that the candidate took the rejection in stride and went on with her work.

As an example:

> *Recently an article I submitted for final approval was rejected for*
> *inadequate research and lack of supporting facts. I thought I had*
> *submitted a superior article. After my initial pouting session, I got*
> *down to work and corrected the shortcomings in the article. My*
> *second submission passed with flying colors.*

7

Leadership

Personality

Confidence

Character

Adaptiveness

Composure

Behavioral

Innovation

Problem Solving

Job Competency

156. Describe workplace innovations you helped develop as a member of a team.

Answer:

The correct response to this question will show how the candidate is able to work as well as a member of a team.

As an example:

You were assigned to a management team with the task of developing an entire new line of interior paint products that included new colors, new textures and at competitive retail pricing. You were able to help the team develop a customer survey that, when completed, showed the team exactly which products customers would desire and would purchase if priced at a good value.

157. Have you had to overcome resistance to change when solving a long-term problem?

Answer:

The answer should include an explanation of how the candidate was able to deal with resistance to change in a business relationship.

As an example:

For many years, the workforce at your work center all took lunch at the same time. This caused the office to completely shut down for one hour each day. This system was causing serious customer service issues. To solve this problem, you implemented a staggered lunch system so there was customer service coverage throughout the entire day. Many people in the office were resistant to the schedule change, but you were able to work with each individual and give them a lunch break they were able to live with.

158. Can you share with us the decision-making protocol that went into your greatest creative achievement?

Answer:

The correct answer to this question should include a decision-making system or protocol the interviewer would recognize.

As an example:

I developed a training program to prepare production workers to safely and efficiently use liquid oxygen in a manufacturing process. I gathered data through direct observation and employee and supervisory surveys. I then plotted the data using project management software. Finally, I led a human resources team in developing, writing, and publishing the training program. The training program is now used industry wide.

159. Do strict deadlines keep you from being creative?

Answer:

This question requires a simple answer about the candidate's viewpoints on deadlines and creativity.

As an example:

If you are not careful, deadlines can put a strain on creativity. I work for a sportswriter for a daily newspaper. In order to keep the presses running, I am required to submit three quality articles every 24 hours. It is not always easy to develop fresh copy. Meeting the deadlines does require me to keep my creative thought processes in action all the time.

160. Are there methods you have developed to motivate yourself to complete undesirable tasks?

Answer:

The correct answer to this question asks the candidate to look deeper into how she responds to difficult tasks. The candidate should provide concrete evidence of self-motivation.

As an example:

I use similar techniques that I would use to motivate another employee to accomplish an undesirable task. I must be able to see the need to get the job done, and to get it done as quickly as possible. I try to schedule as many desirable jobs between undesirable jobs so that my personal satisfaction level stays high.

161. How do you keep track of all your ideas?

Answer:

The correct answer to this question will include a discussion of the candidate's organizational skills as it relates to the development of ideas. Ideas that are not developed have no value to a business or the customers it serves.

As an example:

The candidate may include a description of a journal the candidate is using to document many of the ideas that come to her mind. Other documentation methods include the use of computer software or other electronic devices. To be correct, the candidate must provide some evidence that her ideas are being tracked so they can be implemented at a later date.

162. Do you have an effective method for turning your ideas into actionable elements of a plan, project, or process?

Answer:

To answer this question correctly, the candidate must be able to show he has a track record of making his ideas become a reality.

As an example:

The candidate should be able to provide evidence of taking from his ideas journal and implementing them through a coherent protocol. The candidate may be using a spreadsheet or may be using a word processing program to develop ideas according to a predetermined template.

163. Are there situations in the workplace in which you would not take risks?

Answer:

The correct answers for this question are very serious. It is not acceptable to take unreasonable risks that put human life in jeopardy. It is not acceptable to take risks that jeopardize a coworker's job.

As an example:

If your creative inclination brings you to take an experiment that is very dangerous, and someone gets seriously hurt, you could find yourself in very serious legal difficulties. An unwise experiment could not only be risky to human safety but could also cause serious implications for the company itself.

164. How often do you ask the question "why" at work?

Answer:

The correct answer for a creative person is "often." Creative people should always be asking why things are done a certain way.

As an example:

The boss makes a decision that limits your ability to move forward on a job the way you think it should go, you should be able to respectfully ask if what you are being asked to do does not make sense. Additionally, creative people ask "why?" in another sense. Creative people ask "why?" to open new doors of discovery.

165. Do you often ask why things are the way they are at work?

Answer:

This question is correctly answered by a candidate who understands that many things at work have been done a certain way without anyone really having knowledge of why it is that way.

As an example:

At your job, a certain procedure has been accomplished in a certain way for many years. It seems like no one has ever questioned why the job is being done in a way that really does not seem to make much sense. The candidate should provide a scenario of when she asked "why" at work, and what the outcome was.

166. Are you considered an inquisitive person by your coworkers?

Answer:

The correct answer will cause the candidate to consider whether or not there is a difference between being inquisitive or being simply nosy and getting into other people's way when they are doing their job.

As an example:

An inquisitive worker is someone who is always looking for better ways to do things or trying to make new discoveries. A nosy person asks questions simply to be pesky. This type of person is not a good candidate for most jobs.

167. Are you someone who has been accused of challenging conventional wisdom?

Answer:

The answer the interviewer is looking for is "yes," in addition to an appropriate level of explanation.

As an example:

With the competitive nature of the global marketplace, companies can no longer afford to be stuck in "conventional wisdom." Companies need employees who will ask questions, ignite change and bring about the advances that will provide the competitive advantage needed to maintain profitability. The candidate should be able to provide tangible evidence of times she challenged conventional wisdom.

168. Do you ever impose any personal restraints on your creative thinking?

Answer:

The correct answer should be a qualified "yes."

As an example:

Creative thinking is of no value if there is not recognition of the need to work within the structure established by company leadership. Businesses need employees to be creative, but they also need to follow the direction of the people they work for.

169. Why would you want to work for this company?

Answer:

To answer this question correctly, the candidate should have done her homework. The candidate will need to discuss some of the attributes of the company that are particularly interesting.

As an example:

My research shows that this company is the leading men's clothing retailer in the country. I believe this company would provide me with outstanding opportunities as a designer of men's clothing. I believe I could grow professionally if hired for this job.

170. When was the last time you did something that was really creative?

Answer:

To answer this question correctly, the candidate will need to share a project or an activity he was personally responsible for that other people would be able to look at and recognize its creative value.

As an example:

The company the candidate was working for had an outstanding product that would meet the needs of millions of people, but it was not selling very well. The candidate was given the assignment to design a campaign that included redesigning packaging, television advertising, and advertising in national print media. The result of this campaign was that the sales increased into the millions.

171. **When you were a teenager, did you like to work on your dad's car, or did you want to take a radio apart and see what was on the inside?**

Answer:

This question can be answered correctly regardless of which way the candidate acted as a child.

As an example:

If this is an interview for a job related to the electronics industry, the interviewer will be looking for a candidate who was more interested in taking the radio apart. If this is an interview for a job in a skilled trades industry, the interviewer may be more interested in a candidate who spent his time working on cars. In either case, interviewers are looking for people who are curious about how things work.

172. How do you respond to fans who ask for your autograph?

Answer:

The correct answer is that the performer responds very positively to the needs of the audience. Candidates that refuse to give out autographs may alienate fans.

As an example:

I went to a concert performed by a county band, and after the performance the entire band sat down at a table and signed autographs for every fan who was willing to get in live and wait their turn. This gesture went very far in the effort to build fan loyalty and the profitability of the band.

173. If a team you established came up with a solution to a problem that you disagreed with, what would you do?

Answer:

The correct answer is that I would have to change my position and look at the solution with an open mind.

As an example:

A management team I established to find a solution to our company's losses in the shipping department developed a solution I did not think would work. My first inclination was to overrule the team, but upon further investigation, I realized the wisdom of the solution. I allowed the team's proposed solution to go forward, thus saving thousands in shipping costs.

174. This question is concerned with your organizational skills. What strategies do you use to ensure the project you are designing stays on track?

Answer:

To correctly answer this question, the candidate must be able to establish the fact that he has a system that allows him to keep all of the projects he is working on organized.

As an example:

I personally purchased a software system that provides me with a convenient and efficient means of maintaining my priorities. My goal is to ensure that I meet all of the deadlines that have been established for the projects I am working on. As a result of my efforts, I know each day what I need to get done, I have control over distractions and interruptions, and I have time to attend meetings with clients and staff.

175. When you're working alone on a project at home, how would you rate your ability to get up each morning and be productive?

Answer:

To answer this question correctly, the candidate should be able to affirm he has enough self-discipline to get up each day and complete his work.

As an example:

I get up each day around eight o'clock. After breakfast and a quick shower, I am ready to sit down to whatever project I have for that day. Each day I am working alone, I commit myself to at least six productive hours. The volume of work I have turned in speaks well for my ability to work independently.

176. Once you discovered you had artistic talents, what did you do to develop those talents?

Answer:

I did all I could to learn about different artists, and the techniques they used to complete their work. I eventually went to college and developed my skills to the point I could make a living in an advertising firm.

As an example:

This candidate dedicated her life to a creative career. The quality of her work helped her to receive an invitation to work for a large advertising firm creating images that became part of major advertising campaigns.

177. Please describe something you do on your own initiative to make your work more interesting or exciting?

Answer:

Much of my work is routine requiring little imagination to complete, but I have found some interesting ways to liven up my day.

As an example:

When things at work become boring and difficult to deal with, I take a break and move around the office asking challenging but interesting questions. If I ask the right questions, I can start some very lively conversations. I might even ask questions to solicit advice on a difficult project I was working on.

178. How much guidance do you need from your supervisor to get started on a new project?

Answer:

I am a very well-disciplined self-starter. If I see there is something that needs to be done, I do it.

As an example:

I was given a project that would take me at least two weeks to complete. I could see what steps needed to be taken to get started, and the resources I would need. I completed the project with minimum involvement of my supervisor.

179. Would you consider yourself a self-starter?

Answer:

For most companies, the answer to this question should be a confident yes.

As an example:

The first thing I do when I get to work each day is look around for tasks that need to be accomplished. I am able to work with minimum supervision and do my best to get other people to work the same way.

180. When you are working on creative projects, is there a set of steps you follow to get the project going in a direction that will produce satisfactory results?

Answer:

The correct answer should be yes; I do have a system or program for ensuring my projects move in the right direction.

As an example:

The first step is to use a flowchart to help me identify what I need to do to get the project started correctly. Then I use a project management system to identify the critical path for my project. Finally, I monitor each step to ensure I am receiving the results I need to bring my project to completion.

181. What do you feel is the greatest obstacle you face when working on a project?

Answer:

The interviewer wants to know if you are self aware, and able to identify what obstacles you have at work, and if you are able to resolve them and persevere.

As an example:

I was working with a team on an important project and I found that other people on the team kept saying, "I don't know," and other such stall tactics. I made the team members write down their problems and then held a meeting where all points were discussed which further led to smooth completion of the project.

182. How do you fill your time at work when you do not have any assigned duties to complete?

Answer:

The interviewer typically wants to hear a response that shows them you take initiative to seek out additional tasks or help other team members if you have down time. They may even like to hear that if no one else needs help around the office, that during your downtime you like to find ways to organize, clean up, tie up loose ends on projects, prepare for an upcoming project ahead of time, or even update policies and procedures.

As an example:

When I am sure that all of my assigned work has been completed, and I have time left in the day, I take the initiative and move around the office and look for things to do. It may irritate a few people in the office, but I am committed to setting the example.

183. Did your last employer say there were some ways you could improve your performance?

Answer:

The correct answer should probably be yes. No worker is perfect, and every employer would have something that could be said to someone to help them improve on their job performance.

As an example:

My former employer indicated on my last performance report that my performance was a little short in my ability to work as a team member. The report provided some suggestions for me to improve my performance. I took these suggestions to heart and have made a real effort to be a better team member.

184. What resources do you use to make improvements on your grammar and vocabulary?

Answer:

I am constantly looking at other writer's work, I use a dictionary and thesaurus, I pay attention to the mistakes other people find in my work and I use English grammar books to help me improve my grammar and vocabulary skills.

As an example:

I have a bulletin board near my computer which I use to post reminders of different grammar and vocabulary mistakes I have made. I also post pertinent reminders of the rules of grammar my boss is concerned about. I am working hard to improve my skills.

185. How effective are you at proofreading your own work?

Answer:

The candidate should be able to say she is very good at proofreading her work.

As an example:

It used to be very difficult for me to proofread my own writing. I did not like going back and rereading everything I had written. The newer versions of word processing software have helped me a great deal. The software picks up most of my errors. I also have developed better typing skills, and I am more willing to let other people read my work before I submit it for final approval.

186. When you are writing an article, what methods do you use to keep yourself focused on the particular subject you are writing about?

Answer:

This question is asking the candidate to share some of his personal techniques for maintaining a productive focus. The candidate should share some techniques that sound reasonable to the interviewer.

As an example:

I always try to write on a subject or an angle to a subject that perks my personal interest. It is very hard to write an article on subjects that do not hold your interest. Even if the subject seems uninteresting on the surface, there is usually some interesting angle to the story that can be developed.

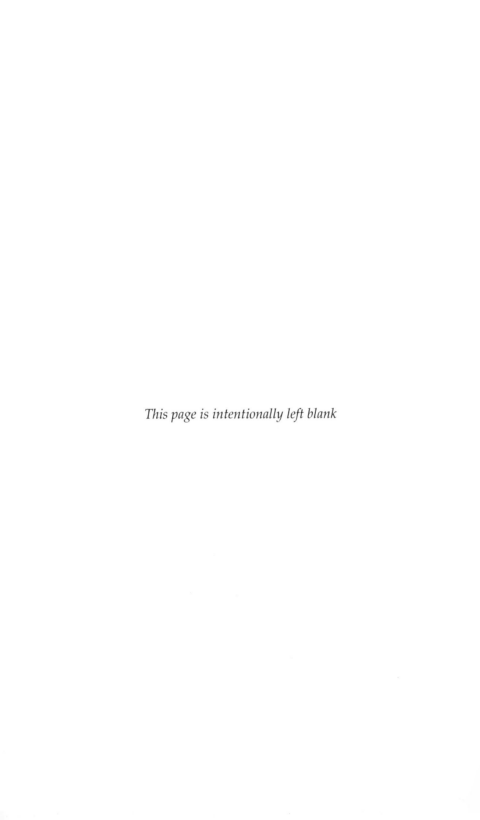

This page is intentionally left blank

8

Leadership

Personality

Confidence

Character

Adaptiveness

Composure

Behavioral

Innovation

Problem Solving

Job Competency

187. **There are times when customers are unhappy with a product and the service provided by your company, and they are expecting a solution that goes beyond normally expected service. Can you share a time when you were able to provide a solution to an unusual customer expectation that made both the customer and management happy?**

Answer:

The correct answer should provide insight into the candidate's attitudes towards meeting customer service challenges. The answer should provide evidence of the candidate's willingness to respond creatively to difficult customers without violating company policies.

As an example:

An important customer from a different time zone needs to regularly conduct business outside of your company's normal business hours. You found a way to extend the time customer service representatives are available without creating the need to increase overtime hours. You were able to meet the customer's needs without creating a financial burden for the company.

188. **Describe workplace innovations you have developed on your own initiative.**

Answer:

The correct answer should provide tangible evidence of the candidate's willingness to take the initiative to solve problems without being prompted by supervisors.

As an example:

Your company was still keeping employee time on paper timecards and you felt you could lead a project to reduce payroll expenses.

As leader of the project, you converted employee time to a fully computerized system that included reporting payroll taxes and fees to the state and federal government, as well as a direct deposit system for the payment of employee salaries. Your efforts saved the company thousands of dollars each year in the costs related to tracking and paying payroll expenses.

189. Have you ever been asked to come up with a solution to a problem that has existed for a long time?

Answer:

In the answer to this question, the candidate is expected to show how she solved a very difficult workplace problem.

As an example:

During the manufacturing processes at your plant, significant amounts of material fall to the floor, causing significant loss to the company. This situation has existed for years. You developed procedures that plant maintenance personnel could follow to recycle as much of the waste as possible, increasing company profitability.

190. Can you think of a situation that required you to think in new or different ways about a problem or project?

Answer:

The correct answer to this question should include a discussion of what the candidate thinks about change and new ideas, and how innovative thinking can be used to benefit an organization.

As an example:

For most of my professional career, I believed that it was essential for effective business accounting to maintain a manual set of books alongside the computerized accounting that was being accomplished. As I discovered, this effort was counterproductive. I learned that if I needed to maintain a hard copy of the accounting that was being accomplished, all I needed to do was request that a hard copy be printed out. The elimination of the manual ledgers saved the company over one million dollars a year in total costs.

191. **In what ways did your expanded ideas, knowledge, or thought processes benefit your employer or business, and can you provide tangible evidence of the benefits?**

Answer:

This question is designed to gain knowledge of the candidate's willingness to learn new approaches to problems or projects.

As an example:

As a professional car salesperson, I have had to learn some lessons the hard way. The downturn in the economy has forced me to become more creative when it comes to finding ways to get customers into an automobile that meets their needs. People are more interested in a vehicle that gives them day-to-day value, than in a flashy car that may not meet all their needs. The end result for me and my employer is that I have been able to meet or exceed all the monthly sales goals set by my manager.

192. Businesses establish organizational processes to control the way they operate and respond to their customer's needs. Can you think of a time when you redesigned an organizational process in response to changing market realities?

Answer:

Since companies operating in the global marketplace are facing the requirement to change organizational processes, the correct answer to the question should include a discussion by the candidate of her ability to assess changing market requirements and creatively bring about the change needed to keep her company profitable.

As an example:

The most important organizational process that I had control over was the processing of customer payments. With the advent of online payment processing, it is essential that our customer's sensitive information be protected, and payments must be applied to customer accounts without error. I directed the purchase and deployment of the software and hardware systems that made these organizational process changes.

193. Organizational structure generally establishes the chain
     of command in a company. New global market realities
     are challenging the effectiveness of the traditional
     organizational structures developed during the 20th
     century. Have you ever been asked to find ways to modify
     a company's organizational structure to meet 21st century
     market demands?

Answer:

This is a serious question that should reveal the candidate's
ability to lead a large corporation. The candidate must be
able to show he is able to provide leadership that will keep a
company relevant in the global economy.

As an example:

*The newer types of organizational structure fall under the
category of virtual and organic systems. Both of these structures
allow businesses and corporations to adjust to changing market
realities in very short periods of time. When I was asked to develop
organizational changes to bring the company into the 21st century,
I conducted extensive research before making recommendations for
change. After collaboration with all of the relevant stakeholders, I led
the company to adopt an organizational structure which provided
significant levels of flexibility.*

194. In your own work experience, have you been able to take
     any creative actions that enhanced creativity, innovation, or
     inventiveness in the workplace?

Answer:

The interviewer is looking for an answer that provides
evidence of the candidate's ability to bring about creative
change in the workplace.

As an example:

The most significant system that I was able to creatively improve was the final packaging of the skateboards our company was manufacturing. Final packaging included promotional materials, labels, instructions, and warnings. Getting each item into the package in the correct order saved the company over one million dollars a year in packaging costs.

195. Can you think of some work you have completed that will have long term benefits to the organization you were working for?

Answer:

Sometimes people do not grasp the long-term consequences of their work. The correct answer to this question should cause the candidate to consider how his or her work created value for the company.

As an example:

My work developing a training protocol for handling liquid oxygen in manufacturing processes will keep thousands of workers safe for many years into the future. Even if changes to the manufacturing process are developed, the principles outlined in the training program can be adjusted and modified to meet current manufacturing realities.

196. What do you believe a company's goals for bringing innovation to bear on the company processes should be?

Answer:

In the 21st century, innovation will be the key to businesses remaining competitive. The advent of modern communications systems provides the means for every person on the planet to be a customer of a company anywhere there is somebody ready to sell something.

As an example:

I updated our company's proprietary software and hardware systems that integrated all of our business processes. The end result of this effort was significant increases in customer satisfaction and company profitability.

197. How often do you present new ideas to your employer or business?

Answer:

The correct answer to this question will reveal just exactly how effective the candidate has been at bringing new ideas that can benefit some business process.

As an example:

The candidate should be able to identify how many ideas she has officially submitted through her company's innovation programs over the last 6 months or over the last year. If the candidate is unable to identify any ideas she has submitted to her last employer, there may be some doubt as to the candidate's commitment to innovation.

198. Can you identify any tangible benefits your ideas have brought to your employer?

Answer:

To correctly answer this question, the candidate will need to discuss how his ideas have increased business profitability, have improved a business process or have improved customer service.

As an example:

In this scenario, the candidate's innovative ideas concerning the realignment of his company's retail floor space led directly to an increase in monthly sales of 25%.

199. How can creativity help a business embrace opportunity of the future?

Answer:

To effectively answer this question, the candidate must display enthusiasm for the future and for all the great opportunities burgeoning in the global marketplace.

As an example:

In this case, the candidate should be able to share information on opportunities she sees in the future that she would be thrilled to be a part of. The candidate may share that the most significant opportunities the future may hold are in the field of computer technology, for example.

200. After seeing how our production processes work, what would you try and change soon after you are hired?

Answer:

Before the candidate could answer this question, he would need a thorough tour of the plant and given the opportunity to think about what was going on.

As an example:

During the plant tour, the candidate notices that some workstations are not aligned in a way that promotes the most efficient use of the worker's efforts. When this question is asked, the candidate can lay out a plan to align workstations so that workers have fewer steps to take during each step of the production process.

---

201. Please describe a situation in which you found a simple solution for a problem that everyone around you thought needed a complex solution.

Answer:

The candidate should provide a discussion of a real work situation in which they solved a problem in a very simple manner.

As an example:

The candidate faced a situation where the company was shorthanded when a very large order came in. Managers needed to get the order filled with a minimum of overtime costs. The candidate found a way to stagger work schedules, so the order was filled without creating significant overtime costs, and the order was filled at a profit.

---

202. How can the chef effectively be involved in the restaurant's marketing and promotional campaigns?

Answer:

The correct answer to this question revolves around the chef's acceptance of the idea that she is at the very center of the restaurant's efforts to market itself to the public. A restaurant will have a difficult time promoting a positive image if people simply do not like the food the chef is preparing each day.

As an example:

Marketing and promotion involves developing a positive brand image for the restaurant. The process may reach far beyond the

doors of the restaurant through radio and television advertising,
print media such as brochures and newspaper advertising.
These administrative duties may force the chef to develop his
communication and marketing skills.

203. Please define for me how you think traditional architecture differs from modern architectural styles.

Answer:

The correct response will include a discussion of the simplicity of modern styles verses the complexity of traditional styles.

As an example:

Today's customer is looking for buildings that allow people to get in, find their way around and at the same time be able to enjoy all of the features and conveniences that advanced technology have created. Advances in construction technology allow architects to explore previously unimaginable design features. The best way to define modern architectural styles is to say, "The sky is the limit."

204. As a member of the news department, have you ever made suggestions for improvement that were accepted? Please tell me the results of the implementation of your ideas.

Answer:

Yes, I have made several suggestions over the last year, and at least one was accepted making significant impact on the quality of the newspaper.

As an example:

I suggested to senior management that we change to a newer version of the publishing software the newspaper was using. The changeover was a significant event because our old computers would not operate with the new software. Although the initial expense was significant, the changeover helped our department put out a much higher quality product.

9

Leadership

Personality

Confidence

Character

Adaptiveness

Composure

Behavioral

Innovation

Problem Solving

Job Competency

205. **Every business faces problems which affect productivity and profitability. Can you share a solution you developed for a workplace problem that was unusual or unexpected, and led to increased productivity or profitability?**

Answer:

The correct answer will provide quantifiable evidence that shows the candidate's efforts increased profitability and productivity.

As an example:

A customer had a large order for an item with specifications slightly larger than the product your company is producing. You are expected to meet this customer's needs without creating increased production costs. In order to keep this customer, you found a way to modify the production process to meet this need without increasing your company's production costs; at the same time, you were also able to meet the customer's price expectations.

206. **Can you describe how your analysis of a workplace problem led to a solution?**

Answer:

The correct answer should provide evidence of the candidate's analytical skills, and the candidate's ability to look at an issue from different angles, developing the best solution to a problem.

As an example:

The employer accelerated production to three shifts per day to meet increased demand for a product and chose not to hire more than five new employees. You found a way to rearrange the existing employee's schedules without creating significant dissatisfaction, and were able to move the five new employees into the schedule in a way they were able to receive the training they needed to be productive workers.

207. **When working in a team environment, are you more willing to assume the creative leadership of the team, or do you allow others to assume the primary leadership position?**

Answer:

In this question, the interviewer is trying to gain an understanding of the candidate's willingness to lead a team's creative efforts. The correct answer will provide concrete evidence of the candidate's creative leadership abilities.

As an example:

The management team you were assigned to had the task of developing new products to reenergize the company's image in the marketplace. It became apparent to you that the process was stalled and not able to move forward in the discovery phase. At a critical point in the process, you stood up and took control of the team's processes and provided guidance that enabled the team to develop the necessary product lines.

208. **Sometimes managers assign different individuals within the company the responsibility to design specific elements of a project. After the different elements have been designed and developed, each individual part will be brought together, making up the overall project. Have you ever been in this type of situation, and how were you able to use your creative skills to bring the whole project together?**

Answer:

In this question, the interviewer is looking for concrete evidence of the candidate's ability to collaborate with other employees on projects.

As an example:

A project you were working on was broken down into five different elements, and your department was assigned to develop one of the five elements of the project. At a predetermined date, the departments were to come together in a single group and meld the five elements into a single cohesive project. Throughout the development of each element, you were required to collaborate with the other four departments so the final project would meld together correctly, and the company could move forward smoothly into production of the total project.

209. **Creative projects are not finished until they are fully implemented. Have you ever had to use your creative skills to overcome obstacles when implementing projects?**

Answer:

The answer should be based upon an actual situation in which the candidate creatively overcame obstacles when implementing a project.

As an example:

As a member of an advertising agency you were responsible for implementing an advertising campaign that included newspaper advertising, as well as radio and television commercials. The client expected all three elements of the campaign to begin the same say. You were able to work with the local newspaper office, radio stations, and regional television networks to ensure the clients requirement for a coordinated advertising campaign were met.

210. Have you ever experienced an emergency situation in which you had to use your creative abilities to solve a very difficult problem?

Answer:

The correct answer will include a discussion of an actual situation that required the candidate to creatively respond to an emergency situation. The interviewer is looking for information that shows the candidate is able to remain calm and operate maturely during workplace emergencies.

As an example:

As an employee of a scientific research company, you are responsible for ensuring perishable specimens are kept at a constant temperature. A violent storm comes through the area causing the loss of electricity and shutting down your company's environmental systems. The emergency generators were not able to support the entire environmental system, but you were able to quickly consolidate the specimens to reduce the load on the emergency power system.

211. What would you do if someone handed you a box of car parts and told you to make the car run?

Answer:

The interviewer is looking for a candidate whose answer demonstrates the ability to organize facts and solve a problem.

As an example:

In order to find out what was going on, I would take all the parts out of the box and lay them out so I could see what I had. I would need to determine which parts were broken or defective. Then I would begin the process of figuring out what needed to be done to get the car running.

212. Can you describe a problem that your supervisor called upon you to solve within the last year that was particularly difficult?

Answer:

To answer this question correctly, the candidate should describe a very difficult problem that was solved to the satisfaction of the supervisor.

As an example:

The candidate was called upon to develop a manufacturing process that would enable the company to save one dollar on each widget that was produced. Since the company produced two million widgets per year, the improved process increased company profits significantly.

213. Please tell me about a time you had to go beyond your expected duties and responsibilities to solve a problem no one else wanted to handle.

Answer:

To answer this question correctly, the candidate will have to reveal a situation when she reached the parameters of her job to solve a difficult problem.

As an example:

I was in charge of the collections department at a major department store, and my responsibilities centered around finding ways to get customers to pay the amount owed on past due accounts. A very unhappy customer had a complaint that the returns department was unable to solve to the satisfaction of the customer. In the absence of the customer service manager, I stepped in and found a way to solve the customer's concern without seriously violating company policies.

This page is intentionally left blank

10

Leadership

Personality

Confidence

Character

Adaptiveness

Composure

Behavioral

Innovation

Problem Solving

Job Competency

214. **Many people are faced with times in their professional and personal life when they are required to take risks to get a project completed on time, overcome emergency situations, or take advantage of a business opportunity. Has there been a situation in your professional life when you had to take a risk to get an important project finished on time?**

Answer:

The correct answer will include a discussion of an actual event in which the candidate had to take a calculated risk to get an important task done by a specific deadline.

As an example:

In order to meet a seemingly impossible deadline, you had to assign a critical task to a team member who had not yet proven himself capable of completing any critical or essential tasks. If the unproven team member failed to get the task done when expected, you would fail to get the overall project completed on time, causing the loss of a profitable contract. In this case, you were able to help the unproven colleague finish the critical task on time, saving the contract for the company.

215. **Please describe any creative work you had with your previous employer.**

Answer:

To answer this question correctly, the candidate will need to provide concrete evidence of his creative work at a previous employer.

As an example:

At my last employer, I was a landscape design planner for the company's residential division. I would go out to the homes of prospective customers, measure their yards, find out their needs and find out what the expected budget for the project should be. I was responsible for designing the project, pricing, building codes, and selling the project to the customer.

216. Can you define the first law of thermodynamics?

Answer:

There are four laws of thermodynamics which describe how different physical elements such as temperature, energy, and entropy interact in nature.

As an example:

*The First Law of Thermodynamics is concerned with the relationship between heat and energy transfer. The Second Law of Thermodynamics is concerned with the relationship between entropy and thermal equilibrium. The Third Law of Thermodynamics is concerned with the relationship between entropy and the temperature of systems. The **Zeroth Law of Thermodynamics** is concerned with the relationship between thermodynamic equilibrium and temperature. Entropy is defined as the process of disorder in any closed system. The Laws of Thermodynamics prove that perpetual motion in machines is impossible to create.*

217. Please name the software programs you are able to use fluently.

Answer:

The candidate may report she is fluent with the Microsoft Office Suite, Java, Oracle, Outlook, Norton, Quicken, Power Point, Excel, and Windows 7 or 8 , to name a few.

As an example:

The candidate should be able to sit down at a computer and pass a test on each software application that he claims proficiency in.

218. Please name the bands or musical groups you have performed with.

Answer:

This question is simple to answer. The candidate should simply name the bands and musical groups she has been a part of.

As an example:

The answer to this question will provide the interviewer with a history of the candidate's musical experience. This history will provide an indication of the musician's skill.

219. Have you written music that has a copyright?

Answer:

The answer to this question is very simple. If the candidate has written and copyrighted some musical scores, then the answer is a simple matter of providing the requested information.

As an example:

If the candidate has been successful at writing music, it is an indication of her musical skill. The group the candidate is applying to will be very interested in the creativity of the musician.

220. Has any of the music you've written been published for public distribution?

Answer:

It would be a great testament of the candidate's musical expertise if he has music being published and sold in music stores. The interviewer will be interested in finding out as much as possible about the candidate's success in the music business.

As an example:

If a musician has music in wide distribution, he or she will have greater employment opportunities. Employers are looking for the highest qualified personnel possible.

221. How did you learn and develop your professional music skills?

Answer:

The candidate should be able to share information about her education, training, and experience as a professional musician.

As an example:

The musician may have studied at a very top-notch university or even the Juilliard School of Music in New York City. After formal training, the candidate should be able to provide evidence of the professional experience he has had leading up to this audition or interview.

222. Who is your primary audience?

Answer:

The correct answer to this question will depend on the style of music the candidate has been involved in.

As an example:

If the musician has been working with symphony orchestras, his audience will be interested in classical music. If the musician works primarily with jazz, then her audience will be people interested in jazz. This evidence will be the key indicator that qualifies or disqualifies the musician for the group he or she is trying to get into.

223. Do you have a good quality instrument?

Answer:

This is a really important question, which seeks some insight into the candidate's ability to adjust to conditions that are less than ideal.

As an example:

Many instrumental performers do not own as good of an instrument as they would like to have. The answer to this question may provide the interviewer with some bargaining power. The interviewer may be able to bring a promising performer into the company with the promise of the opportunity for a higher quality of instrument after a period of time.

224. What is the largest orchestra you have directed?

Answer:

This question is singularly directed at orchestra directors. The person's response to the question will provide information on the professional accomplishments of the candidate.

As an example:

If the candidate has only directed small orchestras, the interviewer will need to determine if the candidate is ready to move up to a larger group. The interviewer may need to see the candidate in action before he can make a hiring recommendation.

225. If you were called to a home to fix a leaking toilet, and you discovered the floor was rotted, what would you do?

Answer:

A good answer to this question would be one in which the interviewer can see you would do your best to ensure the correct repair is made at the most economical price possible.

As an example:

I would figure out exactly what needed to be repaired and immediately provide the homeowner with all of the options available for fixing the problem. I would then work with them on choosing the best option that would solve the problem safely and accurately within their budget.

226. Have you been able to pass the required tests to become a licensed plumber?

Answer:

In most jurisdictions, contractors are required to be licensed to work as a plumber. Passing the tests to become licensed is a measure of the plumber's willingness to be as qualified as possible. If a candidate is unwilling to be licensed, it is a testimony of their lack of professionalism.

As an example:

Working without the required credentials may be a violation of the law. Plumbing companies will be unwilling to hire workers who are unwilling to take the steps required to promote their profession.

227. What was the worst mistake you made as a plumber?

Answer:

To fully answer this question, the plumber will need to share information on a serious mistake she made in a customer's home or business.

As an example:

I was working in a customer's home and I broke open a hot water line, which made water flood the entire first floor of the home. It took me hours to get the leak fixed, get someone to come in and clean up the mess, and make arrangements for my insurance to replace the homeowners damaged belongings. The willingness of the plumber to ensure the customer's losses were covered is a very important issue to the company that may hire this person.

228. Do you have all the specialized tools you need to have as a professional plumber?

Answer:

The correct answer would be a resounding yes! A professional cannot do his job correctly if he does not have the tools needed to do a job quickly and efficiently.

As an example:

If the company sends you out to repair broken water lines under a kitchen sink, do you have the necessary tubing benders, soldering equipment and wrenches to fix the lines in a manner that reduces the customer's inconvenience, and enables us to do the job at the lowest cost to the customer?

229. What skills and talents do you have that make you the very best candidate for this position?

Answer:

To answer this question correctly, the candidate will be required to provide concrete evidence of the value of his skills and talents that qualify him for the position.

As an example:

Depending on which field of endeavor is involved in the particular job opportunity, the candidate will provide information on her education, training, experience and levels of responsibility.

230. Please describe how you view the average day of a chef.

Answer:

If the chef is in charge of the overall operation he will be involved in administration, ordering food and supplies and ensuring everything about the establishment is ready for the doors to open and customers to come in and have a memorable and enjoyable experience.

As an example:

On a normal day a chef may spend time figuring out if he has sufficient food and supplies on hand to prepare every item on the menu that will be presented to the public. He will need to ensure he has sufficient staff scheduled to meet the expected workload, and he will need to ensure the kitchen is a clean and safe place to prepare food for public consumption.

231. What types of food items do you consider to be the areas you specialize in?

Answer:

The chef may say he is very good at pastry dishes, or he may say he is very good at unusual seafood dishes. To answer the question correctly, the chef must be able to show the interviewer he is exceptional in some area of cooking.

As an example:

I am very good at using fresh vegetables from local farms to create dishes that are of interest to the neighbourhood I am working in. Each week I will visit farms in my area to find out what produce will be available, then I will talk to as many people in the area to find out if there are some special dishes they are interested in. In this manner, I make sure the food being prepared at my restaurant will be relevant to the people we hope to draw into the restaurant.

232. Please provide a discussion on the ways a chef can develop his creative talents.

Answer:

People aspiring to be chefs in today's market should begin with some formal training. There are many excellent schools around the country that can provide the basic training a person needs to safely prepare food for the public. After formal training, the aspiring chef should find a kitchen where there is a master chef who is willing to impart his knowledge to someone who is willing to learn.

As an example:

A chef needs to have a fully developed understanding of food combinations that work, of spices that will develop the best taste in a dish and how to put the food on the plate in a way that will enhance the customer's reception of your hard work. After some years of experience, a chef will begin to learn all the ways to impart his personal love and talent into the food he is cooking for his patrons.

233. Please tell me what you think is necessary for a person to be considered a fully qualified architect.

Answer:

In order to be effective when answering this question, the candidate must possess the skills she includes in the answer.

As an example:

As a basis for all that an architect is called upon to accomplish in designing a building or some other structure, he must know building codes, he must know something about structural elements and he must be creative enough to fit the structure being designed into the natural surroundings. A good architect will not violate the environment, nor will he violate the natural surroundings the building must fit into.

234. Have you ever had project management responsibilities on a project you helped to design? If so explain.

Answer:

The candidate may answer yes, he has, or no he hasn't. If the candidate answers in the affirmative, then the interviewer will expect the candidate to elaborate on his experience.

As *an example*:

I was involved in the project management phase on a strip mall complex I had a part in designing. I had to work very hard to separate my two roles on this project. I found it a real challenge not to be offended when construction realities forced some design changes I did not like. I learned some hard lessons during my time working on that project that will serve me well on future projects.

235. Do you have any experience in the actual construction of a building? Please provide some details if you have had some construction experience.

Answer:

The candidate may answer yes, he has, or not he hasn't. If the candidate answers yes, he has construction experience, the interviewer will press the candidate for some details.

As an example:

While I was working on my bachelor's degree, I worked for a company specializing in commercial construction. That real-life experience has been invaluable to me as an architect. I understand fully how my drawings should be tailored to meet construction realties. It does not do me any good to design something that cannot be built.

236. Are you fully qualified as a draftsman?

Answer:

The correct answer is yes. If the candidate is not qualified, he is wasting the interviewer's time.

As an example:

I believe I have become a better draftsman each year over my 15-year professional career. Technology has provided us with some tools that have made the job much easier, but it is still essential in this business to hone your skills as a draftsman. Customers need plans that are well designed and accurately drawn.

237. How would you describe the differences in dealing with the people constructing a project, and the person who is your client?

Answer:

The people who are building my project are primarily concerned with the accuracy of the plans and my willingness to make required changes. The client may have a completely different list of concerns including the financial bottom line, when they can get into the building and how beautiful the final project will look.

As an example:

Construction managers have a primary concern of getting the project built within an established set of deadlines. Clients want to make sure that the project does not go over budget, and that the finished product will meet the needs of the people who will use it.

238. This question requires some advance disclosure by the person conducting the interview. Please share with me a drawing you feel represents your best work.

Answer:

To respond to the question properly, the candidate will need to be prepared to share some of his best work with the interview panel.

As an example:

If the candidate does not have a piece of work to share that is very representative of his work, he will not have an acceptable answer to this request. When the candidate shares his work, he will naturally do his best to describe his work in a positive light. Honesty and transparency will be the best policy.

239. Do you currently have, or will you be able to earn all the certifications necessary for this position?

Answer:

The correct answer is yes, I have the required certifications, and I have a personal plan to gain any certifications I will need in the future to remain qualified in my profession.

As an example:

The most pressing certifications at this point revolve around the issue of meeting environmental requirements. In many jurisdictions, environmental building codes take precedence over many other considerations. I am sure I will be able to meet all of the requirements of the future.

240. Do you have plans to increase your skill and knowledge in architectural design by earning an advanced degree?

Answer:

The interviewer is trying to determine where you see yourself in the future and how far you want to go with your career and education. If you have a degree already, you may want to focus on talking about how you are planning on taking certification courses and keeping up to date on new trends in your field.

As an example:

All candidates should affirm that they are committed to increasing their personal skill and knowledge in the profession. Advanced degrees may not be the correct course of action for each candidate. If a candidate hopes to move into academic pursuits, an advanced degree is essential. Many architects will be able to continue growing professionally without an advanced degree.

241. Are you fluent in the use of computer assisted drafting software?

Answer:

In a professional environment, the answer to this question must be yes.

As an example:

The economic realities of the architectural profession require companies to meet tighter development deadlines. As with any other profession, architects must increase their productivity through the use of computer assisted drafting software.

242. Are there any places in the world that you feel have the greatest opportunities for architects?

Answer:

Up until recently, the construction boom in China offered tremendous opportunities in this profession. Now that the Chinese economy is slowing, companies in the construction industry will need to look to other nations to find the areas of greatest opportunity.

As an example:

I have recently learned that there are some signs of significant growth in the nation of Brazil. I think the major players in the construction industry will need to search the globe for those areas that will offer the greatest opportunities for growth over the next 10 to 20 years.

243. If you had the chance, what would you tell young people who aspire to work in a creative field?

Answer:

This question provides the candidate with the opportunity to share some valuable information on how to prepare for an artistic career.

As an example:

I would tell young people to follow their dreams, but dreams are sometimes only reached through hard work and perseverance. It's not always easy to make a living in an artistic field, and you might not always find success where you planned to go. There are times you will need to go through doors you never expected to be open to you.

244. Have you had success with more than one artistic discipline?

Answer:

If the candidate answers no, that's the end of the question. If the candidate answers yes, then the interviewer will be interested in knowing about the different art forms the candidate has been successful at.

As an example:

The candidate may say that along with her work as a photojournalist, she has had some success as an artist working with oil paint. In fact, some of her artwork has been displayed at the local museum. To the best of the candidate's memory, she has sold five or six of her paintings. This work has helped her to build her confidence and professionalism.

245. Up to this point, have you been working full-time or part-time in a creative field? Please tell me why you want to become a full-time photographer?

Answer:

If the answer is the candidate has been working full-time, the interviewer might ask how the candidate feels about his work up to this point. If the candidate has been working part-time, and wants to move up to a full-time position, the interviewer will be interested in investigating if the candidate is ready to move up into a full-time professional position.

As an example:

The candidate has been working as a freelance photographer making just a few dollars a month. After about five years of this work, the candidate has applied for a full-time position. The interviewer will probably ask for some evidence of the quality of the candidate's work before the hiring process can go any further.

246. As a graphic artist, do you have any special recommendations for people who want to enter your profession?

Answer:

The best recommendation is to find an educational program that will provide you with a sound foundation in the work of a graphic artist.

As an example:

Advancing technology is bringing constant change to my profession. Computer technology is allowing graphic artists to produce increasingly complex images. A good graphic art program will help you to understand the technologies that are driving the profession forward.

247. How effective are you at creating and completing business correspondence?

Answer:

I have excellent business correspondence skills.

As an example:

Just this past year I took a college course on business correspondence and office practices. I passed the course with a typing skill of 60 wpm with 98% accuracy. I fully understand how to use the various business letter forms and have committed very few errors on the letters I submitted to my last boss.

248. Please tell me about all of the different internet sites you have written for?

Answer:

To answer this question correctly, the candidate should have some internet sites he or she has had material published on. If the candidate hasn't written for an internet site and would like to, this is a great time to showcase some goals or aspirations for the future.

As an example:

I have had work published on chron.com, eHowmoney.com, ValuWalk.com and Examiner.com. My work covers a wide range of subjects including family, business and auto repair.

249. What was the primary subject of the articles you have had published on the internet?

Answer:

To answer this question correctly, he will need to provide verifiable evidence of his published work.

As an example:

I have focused recently on business articles such as the following example: Formal vs. Informal Leadership Styles, **http://www.ehow.com/info_12102082_formal-vs-informal-leadership-styles.html**

250. Are you able to write compelling stories for the photographs you take?

Answer:

A professional photographer should be able to indicate to the affirmative that he or she is able to tell a compelling story to go with their photographs. They may need some help, but they should be able to describe the scene successfully.

As an example:

I was assigned to shoot some photographs at the local basketball tournament for disabled middle school students. This activity means a great deal to the young people who were involved. One young man got my attention. It was very hard for him to get the ball up into the basket. I was able to get a photograph at the exact moment he finally made a basket. The look of joy on his face is a picture that I will remember for the rest of my life.

Index

Innovative Interview Questions

Leadership

001. Have you had the sole responsibility of bringing about changes in a company's organizational processes, or did you accomplish this type of change as the member of a team?

002. If you had sole responsibility for bringing about organizational change, how did your co-workers respond to the changes you were trying to bring to the company's organizational processes?

003. Are you able to make a judgment as to whether it is better for an individual or better for a team to bring about organizational changes?

004. As a leader, manager, or supervisor, what creative methods have you personally developed to motivate your subordinates?

005. What methods have you developed to motivate employees to accomplish undesirable tasks?

006. When faced with a subordinate or a peer who is vocally unhappy about accomplishing an undesirable task, what methods have you discovered or developed to mitigate the dissatisfaction and to encourage the person to get the job done?

007. How can company leadership become proactive in identifying employees who have creative talents that would benefit the company?

008. As a manager or corporate officer, have you ever asked the question, "What is our company really good at?"

009. Have you ever asked the question, "What are our company's core competencies?"

010. As a leader, how do you think your subordinates perceive your personality?

011. As a leader, how do you respond to rapidly changing business requirements?

012. Can you tell me about a leadership decision you would like to change now that you have had time to think about it?

013. As a manager or leader, have you had to work on an unexpected assignment over the weekend when you already had plans? How did you handle that situation?

014. If you were in a group of about 10 executives, and you were asked to describe your leadership style, what would you say?

015. How do you deal with the stress that goes along with being in charge?

016. Since the time you moved into executive roles, what has been your most outstanding achievement?

017. As a company leader, have you ever held back from getting involved in an issue knowing you could have made a positive impact on the eventual outcome?

018. How does your background in executive leadership make you qualified for this position?

019. Please tell me one area you need to improve in to become a better leader.

020. Have you built up enough respect for your ideas that people at your last job actually came to you for suggestions?

Personality

021. This question involves risks associated with taking advantage of a business opportunity. Without revealing sensitive personal information, can you describe a risk you have taken to gain an advantage in your business or profession?

022. Has risk-taking helped you grow professionally?

023. Can you say if taking a risk has made you a more creative person?

024. Do you feel the current trends in organizational structure provide sufficient leeway for executives and managers to develop structures that meet current and future needs of businesses operating in the global marketplace?

025. How would you describe or define workplace creativity? Provide concrete examples if possible.

026. How would you describe or define workplace innovation? Provide concrete examples if possible.

027. How would you describe or define workplace inventiveness? Provide concrete examples if possible.

028. In your opinion, how do effective communication skills play into workplace creativity?

029. Do you feel workplace creativity can be taught?

030. If you feel workplace creativity can be taught, what types of classes or activities can be used to accomplish the training?

031. How do you feel workplace creativity influences customer satisfaction?

032. In what ways can increased employee creativity improve a manufacturing company's productivity levels?

033. How important is employee creativity to businesses operating in the global marketplace?

034. Do you think workplaces that encourage creativity are less stressful places to work?

035. Do you consider creativity a skill, a talent, or a little of both?

036. What is your definition of skill?

037. What is your definition of craftsmanship?

038. What is your definition of talent?

039. With sufficient training, do you feel a skilled worker can develop a real talent for a particular task or job?

040. In some workplace situations, employees are closely supervised and allowed little opportunity for individual initiative. In your opinion, are there ways an employee can display creativity in this type of workplace?

041. How do you feel your employers have viewed or judged your creative efforts?

042. It is possible to objectively identify a person with special talents or creativity?

043. Do you think the phrase "thinking out of the box" relates directly to workplace creativity?

044. In your opinion, would you consider yourself innovative or creative, and if so why?

045. Do you feel there is too much or too little emphasis placed on the issue of creativity in the modern workplace?

046. What would you consider are some risks that come from being considered a creative person?

047. Do you think creative people are self-confident?

048. Is it possible for a shy person to begin displaying a creative skill under certain circumstances?

049. What kind of outside forces can cause an organization to become creative?

050. Were you creative as a young child or a teenager?

051. What kind of employer-based incentive do you support as a means to bring out creativity in employees?

052. Is there a creative business you would like to have for yourself?

053. What historical figures do you consider very creative?

054. Which profession has the greatest percentage of creative people?

055. Do you think creative people are given unfair advantages at work?

056. How important is it for senior leadership in a company to surround themselves with creative people?

057. Do you feel your creative talents are great enough to develop ideas that will change the world?

058. What relationship does experimentation have to creativity?

059. Are people conducting statistical research involved in creative activity?

060. Do you ever get tired of being asked about creativity in job interviews?

061. What is it about this job that will get your creative juices flowing?

062. What would you like to say you have accomplished five years from now?

063. What would you like to say you have accomplished 10 years from now?

064. How are the creative talents of a television news producer best developed?

065. How would you describe the creative work of a television news anchor?

066. Can you describe some ways a customer service representative can be creative in her job?

067. What style of music do you enjoy the most?

068. Is there a particular musician that you try to emulate?

069. Which musician had the greatest influence on your development as a professional musician?

070. Please describe what you would consider your ideal job.

071. What would you say are the best things about your present position?

072. Are there any buildings or structures in the world that you particularly admire?

073. Is there a current project this company is involved in that you would like to participate in?

074. Please describe your primary artistic interest.

075. Can you describe your favorite artistic creation?

076. Do you have specific goals for your future endeavors?

077. Do you have any hobbies that are related to your work?

078. Can you tell me about a talent or skill you have that people would be surprised about?

079. At what age or stage in your life did you realize you had artistic talents?

080. Do you consider your work a form of communication, and if so, what kinds of messages are you trying to communicate?

081. How important is good grammar, vocabulary and spelling to an aspiring writer?

082. If we hire you for this position, what are some specific things you hope to accomplish?

083. If you have a choice, are you more interested in taking photographs that tell a human story, or are you more interested in photographs of nature and animals.

084. Do you feel pictures have the power to sway public opinion?

085. Is there a famous sports star that you would like to take a picture of?

Confidence

086. What skills or talents will you bring to the company if we hire you?

087. Please describe the strengths you will bring to this company.

088. How do you think people perceive your music?

089. How do you respond to live audiences?

090. Do you consider yourself fully qualified on the latest advances in construction technology?

091. How do you feel you should be compensated for your creative work?

092. What character traits do you have that make you a great candidate for this position?

093. If we hire you to work as a creative writer, what skills, talents and experience do you bring to the job that are more significant than other candidates have?

094. How willing are you to have a coworker proofread your writing?

095. How do you rate your skills as a researcher?

Character

096. Many people are faced with times in their professional and personal life when they are required to take risks to get a project completed on time, overcome emergency situations, or take advantage of a business opportunity. Has there been a situation in your professional life when you had to take a risk to get an important project finished on time?

097. What lessons have you learned about solving problems when faced with resistance?

098. Of all the projects you have been called upon to complete in your professional career, what would you say was your greatest creative achievement?

099. How important is it that your work on important projects be recognized by professional organizations?

100. If you were an inventor, what kind of device or machine would you like to invent that would make people's lives better or would improve the human condition?

101. Do you desire to have your creative works recognized or publicly displayed?

102. Would you be satisfied with your life's work if you never received any significant public recognition for the work you have accomplished? Please defend your answer.

103. Do you consider a machinist repairing a machine tool in a factory a creative person?

104. Is the auto mechanic who repairs your automobile a creative person?

105. Are engineers who develop software applications simply working as technicians, or are they people who are serving as creative experts?

106. What part of your job makes you wake up with anticipation?

107. How important is safety in the workplace?

108. How would you describe the creative work of a surgical nurse?

109. How would you describe the creative work of a landscaper?

110. How would you describe the creative work of a police officer?

111. How would you describe the creative work of a firefighter?

112. How would you describe the creative work of a welder?

113. When you reach retirement age, what would you like to have people remember you for?

114. Are you good at sharing the applause with the other members of the group you are performing with?

115. What is the greatest thing you hope to accomplish as a musician?

116. Are you willing to perform for charity?

117. Please tell me about the last book you read. What about the book did you find meaningful?

118. How would you define success?

119. Many times people in leadership positions do most of their important work away from the office. What do you think the people who work for you feel about your extended absences from the office?

120. Is there a special reason that you applied for this position?

121. Why do you want to leave your present position and come to work for this company?

122. When do you think it's necessary for a leader to tell workers it is okay to violate established operating standards or procedures?

123. Please discuss your viewpoint on the creative opportunities of a chef.

124. Can you describe how a chef projects the image he is looking for to his staff?

125. Are there any new advances on the horizon that are particularly exciting to you?

126. What has artistic expression brought to your life?

127. As a photographer, what is there about a pristine mountain lake that would cause you to stop and take a picture?

128. If a photographer came upon the scene of a horrific auto accident, how important is it to stop and take some pictures?

Adaptiveness

129. In your experience, are there ways that the requirement to meet strict deadlines can cause you to become more creative?

130. Has there been a situation in your professional life when the requirement to meet strict deadlines stifled your creative efforts?

131. If you had a situation that made it difficult for you to be creative, how did you (or how did you not) overcome the difficulties related to that situation?

132. In response to difficult situations, have you been able to develop some personal strategies for handling similar situations that you may face in the future?

133. As you think back on a failed process or project, have you been able to determine why your creative efforts were not sufficient to bring about a positive result?

134. Successful project management requires managers to be able to look at the direction a project is going and find ways to adjust the project to bring about the expected results. Using a project or business process you have had control over, were you able to find ways to adjust the project to bring about the desired results?

135. Do budgetary limitations imposed by management limit your ability to bring forth innovative ideas?

136. What was the most difficult challenge you ever had to face on the job?

137. Please describe how you would handle a project that had large amounts of conflicting information.

138. How do you respond to interruptions when you are working on critical projects?

139. When you are in the process of designing a building or major project, what are some things that hinder your progress?

140. Have you ever had to collaborate on a complex project with colleagues in remote locations?

141. How does advanced technology help you as an architect?

142. Have you been involved in a project in which you were not provided with enough information to do the job properly?

143. In what ways has modern communication technology changed your job as a writer and communicator?

Composure

144. Can you think of a time when you designed a project or process for your business or organization and the project failed?

145. Please tell me of an instance when you were right, and the boss was wrong?

146. Can you handle more than one creative project at a time?

147. How do you respond when you are accused of making a mistake on a critical project?

148. How do you respond to emergencies or crisis situations?

149. How do you respond to people who are yelling at you about a decision you have made?

150. When you are required to move from project to project throughout the day, how does that affect the way you respond to co-workers and supervisors?

151. What is your response when a co-worker copies your work on a project and tries to take full credit for completing the project?

152. When you are tired and don't feel like working, what do you do to keep yourself sufficiently focused to complete a critical task or project?

153. When you are working on a long and difficult task that never seems to end, how do you keep yourself going all the way to the end of the project?

154. When you are given an overwhelming workload that must be completed by the end of the day, how do you respond?

155. How did you react when your work as a writer was rejected by your supervisor?

Behavioral

156. Describe workplace innovations you helped develop as a member of a team.

157. Have you had to overcome resistance to change when solving a long-term problem?

158. Can you share with us the decision-making protocol that went into your greatest creative achievement?

159. Do strict deadlines keep you from being creative?

160. Are there methods you have developed to motivate yourself to complete undesirable tasks?

161. How do you keep track of all your ideas?

162. Do you have an effective method for turning your ideas into actionable elements of a plan, project, or process?

163. Are there situations in the workplace in which you would not take risks?

164. How often do you ask the question "why" at work?

165. Do you often ask why things are the way they are at work?

166. Are you considered an inquisitive person by your coworkers?

167. Are you someone who has been accused of challenging conventional wisdom?

168. Do you ever impose any personal restraints on your creative thinking?

169. Why would you want to work for this company?

170. When was the last time you did something that was really creative?

171. When you were a teenager, did you like to work on your dad's car, or did you want to take a radio apart and see what was on the inside?

172. How do you respond to fans who ask for your autograph?

173. If a team you established came up with a solution to a problem that you disagreed with, what would you do?

174. This question is concerned with your organizational skills. What strategies do you use to ensure the project you are designing stays on track?

175. When you're working alone on a project at home, how would you rate your ability to get up each morning and be productive?

176. Once you discovered you had artistic talents, what did you do to develop those talents?

177. Please describe something you do on your own initiative to make your work more interesting or exciting?

178. How much guidance do you need from your supervisor to get started on a new project?

179. Would you consider yourself a self-starter?

180. When you are working on creative projects, is there a set of steps you follow to get the project going in a direction that will produce satisfactory results?

181. What do you feel is the greatest obstacle you face when working on a project?

182. How do you fill your time at work when you do not have any assigned duties to complete?

183. Did your last employer say there were some ways you could improve your performance?

184. What resources do you use to make improvements on your grammar and vocabulary?

185. How effective are you at proofreading your own work?

186. When you are writing an article, what methods do you use to keep yourself focused on the particular subject you are writing about?

Innovation

187. There are times when customers are unhappy with a product and the service provided by your company, and they are expecting a solution that goes beyond normally expected service. Can you share a time when you were able to provide a solution to an unusual customer expectation that made both the customer and management happy?

188. Describe workplace innovations you have developed on your own initiative.

189. Have you ever been asked to come up with a solution to a problem that has existed for a long time?

190. Can you think of a situation that required you to think in new or different ways about a problem or project?

191. In what ways did your expanded ideas, knowledge, or thought processes benefit your employer or business, and can you provide tangible evidence of the benefits?

192. Businesses establish organizational processes to control the way they operate and respond to their customer's needs. Can you think of a time when you redesigned an organizational process in response to changing market realities?

193. Organizational structure generally establishes the chain of command in a company. New global market realities are challenging the effectiveness of the traditional organizational structures developed during the 20th century. Have you ever been asked to find ways to modify a company's organizational structure to meet 21st century market demands?

194. In your own work experience, have you been able to take any creative actions that enhanced creativity, innovation, or inventiveness in the workplace?

195. Can you think of some work you have completed that will have long term benefits to the organization you were working for?

196. What do you believe a company's goals for bringing innovation to bear on the company processes should be?

197. How often do you present new ideas to your employer or business?

198. Can you identify any tangible benefits your ideas have brought to your employer?

199. How can creativity help a business embrace opportunity of the future?

200. After seeing how our production processes work, what would you try and change soon after you are hired?

201. Please describe a situation in which you found a simple solution for a problem that everyone around you thought needed a complex solution.

202. How can the chef effectively be involved in the restaurant's marketing and promotional campaigns?

203. Please define for me how you think traditional architecture differs from modern architectural styles.

204. As a member of the news department, have you ever made suggestions for improvement that were accepted? Please tell me the results of the implementation of your ideas.

Problem Solving

205. Every business faces problems which affect productivity and profitability. Can you share a solution you developed for a workplace problem that was unusual or unexpected, and led to increased productivity or profitability?

206. Can you describe how your analysis of a workplace problem led to a solution?

207. When working in a team environment, are you more willing to assume the creative leadership of the team, or do you allow others to assume the primary leadership position?

208. Sometimes managers assign different individuals within the company the responsibility to design specific elements of a project. After the different elements have been designed and developed, each individual part will be brought together, making up the overall project. Have you ever been in this type of situation, and how were you able to use your creative skills to bring the whole project together?

209. Creative projects are not finished until they are fully implemented. Have you ever had to use your creative skills to overcome obstacles when implementing projects?

210. Have you ever experienced an emergency situation in which you had to use your creative abilities to solve a very difficult problem?

211. What would you do if someone handed you a box of car parts and told you to make the car run?

212. Can you describe a problem that your supervisor called upon you to solve within the last year that was particularly difficult?

213. Please tell me about a time you had to go beyond your expected duties and responsibilities to solve a problem no one else wanted to handle.

Job Competency

214. Many people are faced with times in their professional and personal life when they are required to take risks to get a project completed on time, overcome emergency situations, or take advantage of a business opportunity. Has there been a situation in your professional life when you had to take a risk to get an important project finished on time?

215. Please describe any creative work you had with your previous employer.

216. Can you define the first law of thermodynamics?

217. Please name the software programs you are able to use fluently.

218. Please name the bands or musical groups you have performed with.

219. Have you written music that has a copyright?

220. Has any of the music you've written been published for public distribution?

221. How did you learn and develop your professional music skills?

222. Who is your primary audience?

223. Do you have a good quality instrument?

224. What is the largest orchestra you have directed?

225. If you were called to a home to fix a leaking toilet, and you discovered the floor was rotted, what would you do?

226. Have you been able to pass the required tests to become a licensed plumber?

227. What was the worst mistake you made as a plumber?

228. Do you have all the specialized tools you need to have as a professional plumber?

229. What skills and talents do you have that make you the very best candidate for this position?

230. Please describe how you view the average day of a chef.

231. What types of food items do you consider to be the areas you specialize in?

232. Please provide a discussion on the ways a chef can develop his creative talents.

233. Please tell me what you think is necessary for a person to be considered a fully qualified architect.

234. Have you ever had project management responsibilities on a project you helped to design? If so explain.

235. Do you have any experience in the actual construction of a building? Please provide some details if you have had some construction experience.

236. Are you fully qualified as a draftsman?

237. How would you describe the differences in dealing with the people constructing a project, and the person who is your client?

238. This question requires some advance disclosure by the person conducting the interview. Please share with me a drawing you feel represents your best work.

239. Do you currently have, or will you be able to earn all the certifications necessary for this position?

240. Do you have plans to increase your skill and knowledge in architectural design by earning an advanced degree?

241. Are you fluent in the use of computer assisted drafting software?

242. Are there any places in the world that you feel have the greatest opportunities for architects?

243. If you had the chance, what would you tell young people who aspire to work in a creative field?

244. Have you had success with more than one artistic discipline?

245. Up to this point, have you been working full-time or part-time in a creative field? Please tell me why you want to become a full-time photographer?

246. As a graphic artist, do you have any special recommendations for people who want to enter your profession?

247. How effective are you at creating and completing business correspondence?

248. Please tell me about all of the different internet sites you have written for?

249. What was the primary subject of the articles you have had published on the internet?

250. Are you able to write compelling stories for the photographs you take?

Some of the following titles might also be handy:

1. NET Interview Questions You'll Most Likely Be Asked
2. Access VBA Programming Interview Questions You'll Most Likely Be Asked
3. Adobe ColdFusion Interview Questions You'll Most Likely Be Asked
4. Advanced C++ Interview Questions You'll Most Likely Be Asked
5. Advanced Excel Interview Questions You'll Most Likely Be Asked
6. Advanced JAVA Interview Questions You'll Most Likely Be Asked
7. Advanced SAS Interview Questions You'll Most Likely Be Asked
8. AJAX Interview Questions You'll Most Likely Be Asked
9. Algorithms Interview Questions You'll Most Likely Be Asked
10. Android Development Interview Questions You'll Most Likely Be Asked
11. Ant & Maven Interview Questions You'll Most Likely Be Asked
12. Apache Web Server Interview Questions You'll Most Likely Be Asked
13. Artificial Intelligence Interview Questions You'll Most Likely Be Asked
14. ASP.NET Interview Questions You'll Most Likely Be Asked
15. Automated Software Testing Interview Questions You'll Most Likely Be Asked
16. Base SAS Interview Questions You'll Most Likely Be Asked
17. BEA WebLogic Server Interview Questions You'll Most Likely Be Asked
18. C & C++ Interview Questions You'll Most Likely Be Asked
19. C# Interview Questions You'll Most Likely Be Asked
20. CCNA Interview Questions You'll Most Likely Be Asked
21. Cloud Computing Interview Questions You'll Most Likely Be Asked
22. Computer Architecture Interview Questions You'll Most Likely Be Asked
23. Computer Networks Interview Questions You'll Most Likely Be Asked
24. Core JAVA Interview Questions You'll Most Likely Be Asked
25. Data Structures & Algorithms Interview Questions You'll Most Likely Be Asked
26. EJB 3.0 Interview Questions You'll Most Likely Be Asked
27. Entity Framework Interview Questions You'll Most Likely Be Asked
28. Fedora & RHEL Interview Questions You'll Most Likely Be Asked
29. Hadoop BIG DATA Interview Questions You'll Most Likely Be Asked
30. Hibernate, Spring & Struts Interview Questions You'll Most Likely Be Asked
31. HR Interview Questions You'll Most Likely Be Asked
32. HTML, XHTML and CSS Interview Questions You'll Most Likely Be Asked
33. HTML5 Interview Questions You'll Most Likely Be Asked
34. IBM WebSphere Application Server Interview Questions You'll Most Likely Be Asked
35. Innovative Interview Questions You'll Most Likely Be Asked
36. iOS SDK Interview Questions You'll Most Likely Be Asked
37. Java / J2EE Design Patterns Interview Questions You'll Most Likely Be Asked
38. Java / J2EE Interview Questions You'll Most Likely Be Asked
39. JavaScript Interview Questions You'll Most Likely Be Asked
40. JavaServer Faces Interview Questions You'll Most Likely Be Asked
41. JDBC Interview Questions You'll Most Likely Be Asked
42. jQuery Interview Questions You'll Most Likely Be Asked
43. JSP-Servlet Interview Questions You'll Most Likely Be Asked
44. JUnit Interview Questions You'll Most Likely Be Asked
45. Leadership Interview Questions You'll Most Likely Be Asked
46. Linux Interview Questions You'll Most Likely Be Asked
47. Linux System Administrator Interview Questions You'll Most Likely Be Asked
48. Mac OS X Lion Interview Questions You'll Most Likely Be Asked

49. Mac OS X Snow Leopard Interview Questions You'll Most Likely Be Asked
50. Microsoft Access Interview Questions You'll Most Likely Be Asked
51. Microsoft Powerpoint Interview Questions You'll Most Likely Be Asked
52. Microsoft Word Interview Questions You'll Most Likely Be Asked
53. MySQL Interview Questions You'll Most Likely Be Asked
54. Networking Interview Questions You'll Most Likely Be Asked
55. OOPS Interview Questions You'll Most Likely Be Asked
56. Operating Systems Interview Questions You'll Most Likely Be Asked
57. Oracle Database Administration Interview Questions You'll Most Likely Be Asked
58. Oracle E-Business Suite Interview Questions You'll Most Likely Be Asked
59. ORACLE PL/SQL Interview Questions You'll Most Likely Be Asked
60. Perl Programming Interview Questions You'll Most Likely Be Asked
61. PHP Interview Questions You'll Most Likely Be Asked
62. Python Interview Questions You'll Most Likely Be Asked
63. RESTful JAVA Web Services Interview Questions You'll Most Likely Be Asked
64. SAP HANA Interview Questions You'll Most Likely Be Asked
65. SAS Programming Guidelines Interview Questions You'll Most Likely Be Asked
66. Selenium Testing Tools Interview Questions You'll Most Likely Be Asked
67. Silverlight Interview Questions You'll Most Likely Be Asked
68. Software Repositories Interview Questions You'll Most Likely Be Asked
69. Software Testing Interview Questions You'll Most Likely Be Asked
70. SQL Server Interview Questions You'll Most Likely Be Asked
71. Tomcat Interview Questions You'll Most Likely Be Asked
72. UML Interview Questions You'll Most Likely Be Asked
73. Unix Interview Questions You'll Most Likely Be Asked
74. UNIX Shell Programming Interview Questions You'll Most Likely Be Asked
75. Windows Server 2008 R2 Interview Questions You'll Most Likely Be Asked
76. XLXP, XSLT, XPATH, XFORMS & XQuery Interview Questions You'll Most Likely Be Asked
77. XML Interview Questions You'll Most Likely Be Asked

For complete list visit

www.vibrantpublishers.com

NOTES